When Climate Change Hits Home
By Diogo Castro Freire

First published in January 2016

ISBN 978-0-692-61777-9
ISBN 978-0-692-61222-4 (ebook)

Acknowledgements:

I would like to thank Harriett Bobbitt and Margaret Diehl for their help finishing the book, Jordan Koplowitz for the cover, Bill for his support throughout, and the *Adaptation Now* documentary crew (dad, Martha Gregory and Brian Holton Henderson) for our journey together.

I dedicate this book to baby Claire. I hope it makes the world she will inherit a better place.

"Climate change, once considered an issue for a distant future, has moved firmly into the present."

The Third National Climate Assessment[1]
U.S. Global Change Research Program

---

[1] http://nca2014.globalchange.gov/

"Why bother with winter?" said the Grasshopper. "We have got plenty of food at present." But the Ant went on its way and continued to toil.

…

When the winter came the Grasshopper found itself dying of hunger.

Aesop

An extract from the fable "The Ant and the Grasshopper."

Introduction

In late 2015, Pew Research Center asked citizens of countries around the world: "How concerned are you, if at all, that global climate change will harm you personally at some point in your lifetime? Are you very concerned, somewhat concerned, not too concerned or not at all concerned?" In the United States, 30 percent answered "very concerned," relative to a global median of 40 percent, while 29 percent answered "somewhat concerned," relative to a global median of 32 percent.[2]

In other words, the majority of people expressed concern about climate change. These percentages are significant and might come as a surprise to many readers who still expect climate change to be a problem for future generations, but not for them personally. Many people cannot conceptualize how they will be adversely impacted by climate change in the coming years. On the far end of the belief spectrum, some people still see the issue of climate change as a gross exaggeration of normal shifts in weather, a delusion, or a conspiracy by scientists looking for attention and grant money. Luckily, they are the minority.[3]

Nonetheless, it shocks me that in late 2015 the majority of people expressing concern is still so slim and that many of them are only "somewhat" concerned. There is a clear disconnect between public opinion and the scientific consensus. In sharp contrast to public opinion, nearly 100 percent of climate scientists agree climate change is real, manmade, and a *BIG* problem.[4]

---

[2] http://www.pewglobal.org/2015/11/05/global-concern-about-climate-change-broad-support-for-limiting-emissions/
[3] More information on evolving climate change beliefs can be found at the website for the Yale Project for Climate Change Communication: http://environment.yale.edu/climate-communication/
[4] http://climate.nasa.gov/scientific-consensus/

Introduction

I spent the last year of my life launching a documentary project called *Adaptation Now* on how climate change is starting to impact US communities: a somber topic.[5] I pulled the trigger and started writing this book for the same reasons I felt compelled to make the documentary. First, I was astonished by the number of people who had already been adversely affected by climate change. Second, it was painful to learn how many of them were completely caught off guard when disaster hit. Finally, it was alarming to see how inadequate some of the communal responses to these climate disruptions have been.

Having studied the subject of climate change for several years, it is clear to me there is much we can do to address it. This is one of the most frustrating points. The main obstacle to meaningful progress is not technological or economic; instead, it is a lack of basic awareness. Much of the research for the documentary has been recycled and used as the bedrock for this book, which I see as a complementary effort. The goal of both the documentary and the book is to raise what I call *productive awareness* by:

- Explaining the issues in a way that makes them real.
- Providing direction and guidance to the people inspired to act on them.

Along the way it has been my privilege to engage with a large number of commendable individuals and organizations working arduously to solve climate change. Coming from all walks of life, they are united by a common sense of purpose, urgency and determination. They feel compelled to address what might be the defining challenge of our generation. Luckily for all of us, their numbers continue to rise, with more climate advocates joining the cause every day. As with the documentary, I hope this book amplifies their voices and helps them scale their efforts.

---

[5] http://www.adaptationnow.com/

5

Introduction

Pope Francis dominated press and social media coverage last summer when he put out a strong call for action on climate change in his encyclical, *Laudato Si': On Care for Our Common Home*. "The urgent challenge to protect our common home includes a concern to bring the whole human family together to seek a sustainable and integral development, for we know that things can change," he wrote.[6] His words have caused a measurable and significant change in people's perceptions of climate change. The Yale Project on Climate Change Communication studied the effect and found that 17 percent of Americans were influenced by the pope's views. After the publication of the encyclical, the percentage of Americans worried about climate change grew by 8 percentage points.[7]

This is an extremely positive development, but the journey ahead is still long and uphill. In a strategy class at the Harvard Business School, my professor asked, "How do you shoot a bird?" Ted raised his hand and replied, "With a shotgun." Ted wasn't wrong, but the professor's response refined the problem in the following way: "You need to aim at where it's going, not where it is." We make decisions based on our expectations for the future. This becomes practically automatic when situations are sufficiently repetitive. A very basic example is that you can plan for a meal long before you are actually hungry; you have come to expect becoming hungry at certain times of day or a few hours after a meal. When we face new situations, on the other hand, our ability to accurately predict the future is compromised.

To be more precise, the conditions required for developing good intuition are: "an environment that is sufficiently regular to be predictable" and "an opportunity to learn

---

[6] http://w2.vatican.va/content/francesco/en/encyclicals/documents/papa-francesco_20150524_enciclica-laudato-si.html
[7] http://environment.yale.edu/climate-communication/article/the-francis-effect/

Introduction

these regularities through prolonged practice." If, on the other hand, the "quality" and "speed" of feedback is limited, people are unlikely to develop skilled intuition. This eloquent depiction of how our brains develop intuition was authored by Nobel Prize-winner Daniel Kahneman in his 2011 masterpiece, *Thinking Fast and Slow*.

Our climate has been fairly stable for millennia, driven by the complex interplay of a seemingly endless list of variables that can take years to understand. This partially explains why, as you will notice throughout this book, we remain largely unprepared when it comes to climate change. For many people, the reality of climate change is something they haven't mentally processed yet. They haven't connected the dots between the planet's warming and what that personally means for them.

In his book *The Politics of Climate Change* (2011), Lord Anthony Giddens tries to summarize some of the social and cognitive biases that impair our response to climate change in a concept he calls "Giddens's Paradox." He describes the paradox thusly: "...since the dangers posed by global warming aren't tangible, immediate or visible in the course of day to day life, however awesome they appear, many will sit on their hands and do nothing of a concrete nature about them. Yet waiting until they become visible and acute before taking serious action will, by definition, be too late." To make his point, Giddens uses the analogy of a healthy teenager who develops a smoking habit despite the onslaught of warnings shouting "SMOKING KILLS!" As Giddens explains, "People find it hard to give the same level of reality to the future as they do to the present ... for a teenager, it is almost impossible to imagine being 40, the age at which real dangers start to take hold..."

George Marshall explores this topic in greater depth in his 2014 book, *Don't Even Think About It: Why Our Brains Are Wired to Ignore Climate Change*. Throughout the book, he tries to decipher why "... most of us recognize that climate change is real yet we do nothing to stop it." Marshall brings to life many of the core behavioral traits we've developed as our species has evolved. In the chapter entitled "The Invisible Force Field of Climate Silence," he demonstrates how – in order to avoid anxiety and uncomfortable conversations – most people simply choose not to engage on this topic.

Applying our understanding of psychology and sociology to climate change, Marshall uncovers why it has lingered for so long in our communal blind spot. As he puts it, "Without doubt, climate change has qualities that play poorly to these (our) innate tendencies. It is complex, unfamiliar, slow moving, invisible, and intergenerational."

Further aggravating the situation are active disinformation campaigns. In the 2010 book (and now film) *Merchants of Doubt*, professor Naomi Oreskes and historian of science Erik Conway reveal the striking and shocking similarities between the tactics used by fossil fuel companies to stall meaningful action on climate change to those used by tobacco companies in the late 20th century. On both occasions, these companies resorted to sponsoring contrarian studies and spokespeople from seemingly independent institutions. The goal was simple: to create the perception of uncertainty regarding the science in order to sow doubt among the general public. It is a similar approach to that of a defense attorney introducing doubt into jurors' minds so that her client gets away with murder.

These campaigns are not based on the pursuit of scientific knowledge, nor do they uphold the standards and rigor of scientific research. They seek, instead, to exploit the vulnerabilities of human sociology and psychology. The documentary TV series *Years of Living Dangerously* explores this topic in depth in its episode "Winds of Change." Correspondent America Ferrera follows the work of – and uncovers the tactics deployed by – a now well-known player in this arena of (un)truth, James Taylor of the Heartland Institute. Taylor, a gifted and persuasive speaker, is found exaggerating his scientific credentials and confidently presenting cherry-picked data to politicians.

Such was the embarrassment resulting from these types of campaigns that in 2015, Royal Dutch Shell, one of the world's biggest oil and gas companies, publicly announced it would not renew its membership with the American Legislative Exchange Council (ALEC). A Shell spokesman stated, "We have long recognized both the importance of the climate challenge and the critical role energy has in determining quality of life for people across the world. As part of an ongoing review of memberships and affiliations, we will be letting our association with ALEC lapse when the current contracted term ends early next year."[8]

With this as context, now consider some of the many things we rely on that are influenced by weather: water supply, crop yields, immune system response, electricity power production, traffic conditions, flight cancellations... All it takes is a little thought to realize how our climate can wreak havoc. If greenhouse gas emissions continue unabated, climate change (which we are already experiencing) will fundamentally disrupt countless lives. But if the majority of people are not yet paying attention to the noticeable shifts and underlying trends in the weather, we may conclude that many people are making avoidable mistakes. Some of these mistakes will, it grieves me to say, cause tremendous pain and have far-reaching ripple effects. Those ripples will touch me, you and yours.

Where would you like to build your dream home? What kind of community do you want to be a part of? Where would you like to raise your family? Where would you like to grow old and enjoy the spoils of decades of hard work?

---

[8] https://www.washingtonpost.com/news/post-politics/wp/2015/08/07/shell-oil-will-drop-its-membership-in-alec-citing-differences-over-climate-change/

Introduction

Perhaps you've already made these choices. In any case, the last time you tried to answer these questions did you think about how climate change would affect matters? Did you factor in how it may change the desirability or feasibility of your options?

Making a home is, for most of us, the single biggest investment of our lives. It's not just a financial investment; it's an emotional one. Home is where we spend most of our time on this Earth. For this reason, I devote a great deal of attention in this book to the impacts of climate change on property. It is an issue grossly neglected by the majority of prospective buyers and, to a lesser extent, sellers.

The broader theme, developed across 7 chapters, involves how we begin to prepare for climate change – as individuals, families and communities. My ultimate goal is to empower you with the right mindset, knowledge and resources to reduce your exposure to climate change risks. What happens afterwards is up to you.

Contents

Chapter 1 - The Basics

Fossil fuels are a pillar of the modern economy. To a large extent, this has been a good thing. Since the industrial revolution, we have built a civilization that is, while far from perfect, more prosperous and full of opportunity than anything before it. We owe a great deal of thanks to the generations of people whose efforts brought us coal, oil, and gas. Some of them risked or lost their lives to bring us these energy-rich fuels that have powered the world we know today—a world of global travel, fantastic advances in science, medicine and technology, a larger middle class, longer lives, and better health, nutrition and education for billions of human beings.

We now know that burning fossil fuels, deforestation (which releases the carbon locked in the wood) and certain farming practices increase the concentration of greenhouse gases (GHG) in the atmosphere, not just for a little while, but for decades and centuries (depending on the gas). We also know a great deal about the properties of these gases and their impact on global climate trends. This knowledge is why climate change is increasingly a priority for world leaders and, as time goes by, for people like you and me.

The physics and chemistry of climate change are relatively simple to explain. A greenhouse gas like carbon dioxide, the most prevalent one in our atmosphere, has the physical property of trapping heat. This property can be tested and demonstrated in high school labs. As the concentration of carbon dioxide in the atmosphere increases, more heat is trapped, causing average temperatures to go up. The majority of CO_2 dissolves into the ocean within 20-200 years. The rest can take up to hundreds of thousands of years to dissipate. Methane, the second-most dangerous gas, lasts only about twelve years, but is 84 times more potent than CO_2 at trapping heat. Since there is comparatively little methane in the atmosphere at present, it attracts less attention. (Some scientists do worry about methane released from permafrost and the ocean floor as the planet warms. Methane is also a natural product of the digestive system of cattle.)

The warming of the planet does not mean that we are going to stop experiencing winters altogether or that we will no longer have extreme cold weather events. What we are talking about is a shift in the baseline, the underlying mean. Extreme cold weather will still be possible, but on average we will have higher temperatures. The astrophysicist Neil deGrasse Tyson explains this well in an episode of the TV docuseries *Cosmos*, a production dedicated to explaining climate change. He walks in a straight line, holding a dog on a leash. Unlike deGrasse Tyson, the dog runs around in all directions freely and sporadically. Tyson uses this analogy to explain the difference between changes in climate and the weather. Tyson walking on the straight line is the equivalent to global warming; it is a consistent trend. The dog's movements are representative of the weather... volatile, sporadic and subject to extremes, but always anchored by Tyson's hand on the leash.

This relationship has held true in the past and, indeed, it holds true today. Average global temperatures go up and down with carbon dioxide levels. Sometimes there are time lags; additionally, the interplay of climate variables can produce interesting and unexpected results. The underlying direction, however, is clear and continues to hold steady.

In the mid-1800s, John Tyndall became the first person to demonstrate in a lab the heat- trapping properties of carbon dioxide. At the time, Tyndall was trying to determine why glaciers changed in size. Assuming that the culprit was the atmosphere, he built a device to test whether gases could trap heat and light. Confirmation of his theory was a major scientific breakthrough. Three decades later, Svante Arrhenius connected the dots and claimed—for the first time—that fossil fuel combustion could cause global warming. He made an initial attempt to quantify the correlation between global temperatures and the amount of CO_2 in the atmosphere. Apparently his initial calculations, formulated without the use of today's advanced models, are within range of modern forecasts.

In fact, scientists have been proving Arrhenius' claim ever since and there is mounting evidence. Unfortunately, whichever way we look at the problem, we arrive at the same conclusion... a conclusion many of us, myself included, wish were simply not true. A cornerstone of climate science is Keeling's Curve, which is based on readings from the Mauna Loa meteorological observatory in Hawaii. Charles Keeling, a man described as "obsessed" with the study of CO_2, developed an instrument to measure its concentration. He took it to Hawaii, away from polluted air, to get clean readings. The results showed a rapid increase of CO_2 concentration in the late 20th century.

In 2015, we were responsible for emitting over 30 billion metric tons of CO_2.[9] To put this in perspective, an adult male African elephant weighs about 5 tons. We are currently dumping in the atmosphere the CO_2 equivalent of 6 billion elephants every year. They plan on staying up there a very long time.

How do we know what levels are safe? To answer this scientists have closely examined what is essentially pre-historic data. Using air bubbles trapped in ancient glaciers and in the planet's polar ice sheets, scientists can obtain temperature and GHG records going back almost a million years. The records confirm the strong causal relationship between carbon dioxide concentration and temperature. Confirmation can also be found in the study of tree rings

---

[9] http://www.bbc.com/news/science-environment-31872460

and fossils, among other data sources allowing us to travel back in time.

More recently, satellite technology has corroborated the expected trend based on historical data. The increase in CO2 has led to a noticeable decline in the amount of energy radiating from the Earth back into space. NASA has "nearly 30 years of satellite-based solar and atmospheric temperature data," and the numbers don't lie.[10] These and other studies have enabled the development of increasingly sophisticated forecasting models. The models substantiate the predictions, made by pioneering scientists over a century ago, of what are now measurable and visible trends.

The Earth's temperature is rapidly increasing as a direct result of our emissions and omissions. In the United States, average temperatures were 1.3°F to 1.9°F warmer in 2014 (when the National Climate Assessment was published) than in 1895 (when records began).[11] Alaska, as an example, has been warming at more than double the national rate! On a global level, the 10 hottest years on record were all after 1998.[12] The hottest year on record was 2014, an "El Nino" neutral year; in other words, the 2014 temperatures were not subject to the natural warming variability caused by El Nino. 2015 is expected to claim this title for itself. I suspect it won't manage to hold it for very long.

As can be reasonably expected, world leaders have wanted to be absolutely certain about this. The implications of climate change mitigation are profound, second only to letting climate change proceed unabated. As such, much work has been done to ensure that the cause of manmade climate change is, in fact, emissions. Scientists have

---

[10] http://climate.nasa.gov/nasa_role/
[11] http://nca2014.globalchange.gov/highlights/report-findings/our-changing-climate
[12] http://www.arctic.noaa.gov/detect/global-temps.shtml

looked at all other possible alternatives, chief among them, solar irradiance. Their findings have been consistent; no other variable is a plausible cause for the observed trends. Remove CO_2 from the models, and the measured temperature increases make no sense. NASA has been actively tracking the sun's energy output since 1978, finding that solar irradiance in the last 30 years has actually gone down.[13]

A few years ago, the scientific consensus was that we should limit the amount of carbon dioxide in the atmosphere to 350 parts per million. This is what many refer to as the "safety threshold." Today, we find ourselves at 400 parts per million, adding another 3 parts per million every year. This rate is itself increasing. The only thing that has managed to slow its growth is the occasional economic downturn. Comparing these values to the historical range helps us understand why this is problematic. For at least 800,000 years, CO_2 levels have oscillated (gradually) from lows of about 180 parts per million (that coincided with ice ages) to highs of about 280 parts per million (during the warmer interglacial time periods). In short, for 800,000 years they have never exceeded 300 parts per million.

Let me reiterate. In 2015, we were already at 400 parts per million.

For hundreds of thousands of years, a change of 100 parts per million was the difference between a tropical planet or one covered in ice. It's not the end of the world... this planet has experienced even larger concentrations of CO_2 further back in time. Different geologic eras have supported different kinds of life—as the Arctic and the Equator do now—and most of those eras could have supported human life, had we been around to enjoy them. The problem is the scale and pace of change, and what that means for both human life and the biodiversity we

---

[13] http://climate.nasa.gov/causes/

depend on. A relatively stable and predictable climate helps us prosper; conversely, an unstable one is incredibly disruptive.

My wardrobe in San Francisco looks very different from its predecessor in Boston—both winter coats and summer shorts are of little use to me now. I can change my wardrobe at a reasonable cost and, fortunately for me, relocation is something I can afford. But that doesn't make me immune to more dramatic and permanent shifts in climate. FEMA called Hurricane Katrina the "single most catastrophic disaster in US history." It is a dreaded reminder of what happens when nature stresses and breaks the limits of our physical and social infrastructure. The city's levees built by the Army Corps of Engineers suffered multiple breaches. Floodwaters poured in, trapping and drowning thousands. Emergency services struggled to respond. Law and order broke down.

There are limits to how much change we can withstand. All of us plan our lives and build our homes expecting some (limited) degree of variability, even if we don't think about it. This is true on multiple fronts—from the physiological comfort of the individual, like my personal lack of tolerance for heat and cold, to the reliability of the shared infrastructure that brings water and power to our homes.

The science of climate change is not up for debate. The International Panel on Climate Change (the IPPC) is an unprecedented effort to combine scientific knowledge and expertise from around the world and periodically publish a document that sets out the consensus understanding. In November 2014, all 195 member national governments of the IPCC approved the Summary for Policy Makers report, which summarizes the scientific community's position on climate change: "Warming of the climate system is unequivocal, and since the 1950s, many of the observed changes are unprecedented over decades to millennia. The atmosphere and ocean have warmed, the amounts of snow and ice have diminished, and sea level has risen… Anthropogenic (manmade) greenhouse gas emissions … are extremely likely (95% probability) to have been the dominant cause of the observed warming since the mid-20th century." Stanford University Professor William Anderegg surveyed the world's leading climate scientists to further confirm this consensus. In his study, Expert Credibility in Climate Change, he found that an overwhelming 97 percent agree! Also demonstrated by the survey's results was that "the relative climate expertise and scientific prominence" of the 3 percent that didn't agree was noticeably less than that of the 97 percent that did agree. At the time of this writing, NASA has an online list with the leading scientific institutions around the world that support these conclusions; that list includes everyone from the US National Academy of Sciences to the UK Royal Society.[14]

As I said, there is no debate. There is no reputable scientific institution that disputes any of these facts. If you find one, let me know! Even the biggest oil companies publicly recognize the threats:

"Meeting energy demand is a massive challenge. But so too is the need to tackle the real and growing threat that climate change poses."

Ben van Beurden, CEO, Royal Dutch Shell
Speech at Center for Global Energy Policy,[15] September 2014

"ExxonMobil takes global climate change seriously and the risks of rising greenhouse gas emissions warrant thoughtful action."

---

[14] http://climate.nasa.gov/scientific-consensus/
[15] http://www.shell.com/media/speeches-and-articles/2014/working-together-to-build-a-lower-carbon-higher-energy-future.html#vanity-
aHR0cDovL3d3dy5zaGVsbC5jb20vZ2xvYmFsL2Fib3V0c2hlbGwvbWVkaWEvc3
BlZWNoZXMtYW5kLWFydGljbGVzLzIwMTQvd29ya2luZy10b2dldGhlci1sb3dlci1j
YXJib24taGlnaGVyLWVuZXJneS5odG1s

The Basics

Ken Cohen, VP of Public and Government Affairs, Exxon
Mobil
Exxon Mobil Perspectives,[16] May 2015

All of the other oil and gas majors (Chevron, BP, Conoco, Total) have publicly stated similar positions. Exxon, in particular, has been well aware of the dangers of CO2 buildup for a long time, long before they made their current position public.[17] Exxon funded major studies in the 1980s to explore the threat of climate change, with its scientists openly publishing their findings in peer-reviewed papers.

As temperatures increase, our lives become increasingly complicated. We now face new and ugly risks, some already noticeable, as evident in The National Climate Assessment. This study was conducted in the United States, with multiple federal agencies collaborating. Among them were the Departments of Defense, Energy, Agriculture, and Commerce, as well as National Oceanic and Atmospheric Agency (NOAA), NASA, the National Science Foundation, the Smithsonian Institution and the Centers for Disease Control and Prevention (the CDC). We are not only talking about events that will take place in the coming decades. We are talking about a clear and present danger. Below is a powerful extract from the summary report: "Changes in extreme weather and climate events, such as heat waves and droughts, are the primary way that most people experience climate change. Human-induced climate change has already increased the number and strength of some of these extreme events. Over the last 50 years, much of the U.S. has seen increases in prolonged periods of excessively high temperatures, heavy downpours, and in some regions, severe floods and droughts."

---

[16] http://www.exxonmobilperspectives.com/2015/12/02/exxonmobil-on-the-u-n-climate-talks/

[17] http://insideclimatenews.org/content/Exxon-The-Road-Not-Taken

The Basics

Understanding the full ramifications of climate change is a difficult task because of the complexity of the Earth's climate – there are many variables that influence each other, making, as previously mentioned, the very nature of weather chaotic. We have gotten better over time, nonetheless, at what scientists call "attribution" and continue to do so. In this context, attribution means determining the contribution of manmade GHG emissions to weather events. Scientists use statistical models to determine what events fall within or outside of natural variability. They then compare the results with what is expected given higher concentrations of GHGs in the atmosphere.

The devastating 2012 surge from Superstorm Sandy is an example that is easy to grasp. Sea levels are higher today along the East Coast of the United States. The difference in height has a discernable impact on how far and how high a storm surge goes. The science team behind the documentary TV series *Years of Living Dangerously* estimated that in New York City alone 75,000 additional people were affected as a result of sea level rise. As is commonly said, "Seeing is believing." If you are, in fact, looking for more visual confirmation of rising seas, I encourage you to watch the documentary *Chasing Ice.* The world's glaciers are disappearing at an alarming rate and the crew behind this beautiful film has done us the great service of documenting their retreat. It is estimated that over 90 percent of glaciers worldwide are retreating.[18] When last measured, the rate of retreat had accelerated.

As we observe each time we boil water, higher temperatures cause more evaporation. They also increase the amount of vapor the air can hold. It follows that we will experience simultaneously worse droughts and storms, caused by more evaporation and more vapor in the air, respectively. Tracking and studying droughts and storms

---

[18] http://www.theguardian.com/environment/2010/jan/20/climate-change-glaciers-melting

over the past decades have allowed scientists to confirm that this is, indeed, the case. Conforming to this trend, Hurricane Patricia (2015) was the strongest hurricane ever! In recent years, several parts of the US have suffered severe drought conditions—Texas and Oklahoma in 2011, California from 2012 until (perhaps) the end of 2015. In some cases, showing clear deviations from historical norms, "... rates of water loss were double the long term average." Simultaneously, there has been an increase in the amount of rain falling in "heavy downpours." The statistics are impressive, with the Northeastern United States having seen a 30 percent increase in heavy downpours relative to the average.[19]

At a conference in DC in the summer of 2015, Dr. Katharine Hayhoe, a renowned climatologist working at Texas Tech University, reminded the audience that roughly "7 billion people now live on the planet and two thirds of the world's largest cities are within two feet of sea level."[20] What she was hinting at is that we are on a trajectory for mass migration on an unprecedented planetary scale. The World Bank estimated in 2015 that by 2030 an additional 100 million people could be pushed into extreme poverty on account of climate change; the drivers would include natural disasters, agricultural shocks and deteriorating health conditions.[21]

Unfortunately, this is happening at a time when migration is increasingly difficult. In 2015, Europe's migrant crisis garnered widespread media attention as multiple ships carrying thousands of migrants sank in dangerous attempts to cross the Mediterranean. European governments struggled to cooperate in finding a resolution. Record numbers of migrants escaping instability in the

---

[19] http://nca2014.globalchange.gov/highlights/report-findings/extreme-weather
[20] The 2015 Citizens' Climate Lobby International Conference, Washington, DC, June 2015
[21] http://www.worldbank.org/en/news/feature/2015/11/08/rapid-climate-informed-development-needed-to-keep-climate-change-from-pushing-more-than-100-million-people-into-poverty-by-2030

Middle East and Africa continue to flee to Europe's closed borders. It is the perfect example of how we remain unprepared for mass migration. Historically, we've done quite poorly across the world at helping displaced people. The Office for the United Nations High Commissioner for Refugees (UNHCR) estimated that, in the early 2000s, the average amount of time people spent in refugee camps had increased to almost two decades![22]

Predicting the full domino and knock-on effects of climate change is hard. One public study called Risky Business, co-chaired by, among others, former Treasury Secretary Hank Paulson and former Mayor of NYC and billionaire Michael Bloomberg, estimates the economic losses from climate change at a regional level and finds them substantial. The study anticipates declining labor productivity across entire regions, such as the southeastern United States, which has been battered by floods and extreme heat in recent years. They estimate that, by midcentury, the region will experience an increase in the average number of extremely hot days (with temperatures 95 or above) of 17 to 53 per year from a baseline of 9 today.[23] Vulnerable sectors include construction, agriculture, transportation, manufacturing, mining and utilities.

Personally, I'm utterly useless when it gets too hot and equally useless when it gets too cold. With my *"petite nature"* (little nature), any slight temperature change triggers immediate sneezing. It's a constant reminder of how frail our bodies actually are. We may be an adaptable species, but there seems to be no end to the number of things that need to be just right in order for us to be our best selves.

One of my favorite analogies for understanding the risks of small changes to global temperature is the now commonly

---

[22] http://www.unhcr.org/4444afcb0.pdf
[23] http://riskybusiness.org/

used body temperature analogy. If our body temperature goes up by just one degree, we already start feeling a little off. At two degrees, we feel really sick and our bodies start behaving in very weird ways, from profound sweating to shivering and muscle aches. Beyond two degrees we are at risk of actual death. It is an ironic coincidence that scientists have defined two degrees warming as the safety threshold of tolerable risk for climate change. The World Health Organization estimates that today (2015) there are at least 150,000 annual deaths worldwide that can be attributed to climate change, but most people fail to see the connection.[24] The TV series *Years of Living Dangerously* did a good job of explaining the threats of "thermal stress." In the episode "Mercury Rising," Matt Damon interviews experts tracking the substantial increase in mortality rates across major US cities during heat waves. He reports something most people don't realize: the death toll from heat in the US exceeds that of hurricanes, floods, tornadoes and earthquakes combined. Most at risk are the old and the very young.

So what happens as climate change continues unchecked and these effects amplify? The United States Department of Defense summarized it well in its 2014 *Climate Adaptation Roadmap*: "Among the future trends that will impact our national security is climate change ... Rising global temperatures, changing precipitation patterns, climbing sea levels, and more extreme weather events will intensify the challenges of global instability, hunger, poverty, and conflict." In other words, if we continue with our current emissions trajectory, lives will be lost.

Let's take a step back from this ugly prognosis and start thinking in terms of action. It's time to take control of the situation. The chapters that follow help answer three essential questions: How do we reduce exposure to these risks? How do we reduce the level of risk? How do we stop climate change altogether? Unlike most books on this

---

[24] http://www.who.int/heli/risks/climate/climatechange/en/

topic, the emphasis here is on the power of the individual and the power of community. Yet I'm not just going to ask you to change your light bulbs and call it a day. I'm also not going to ask you to adopt a completely different and regressive lifestyle. There is no time for half-baked or unrealistic solutions.

Chapter takeaways:

- There is an irrefutable scientific consensus that climate change is real and manmade.
- The threats of climate change are substantial, not only to the economy, but— more importantly—to human life.
- The impacts of climate change are already being felt today in multiple forms, from increased heat waves and droughts to heavy downpours and material sea level rise.
- Oil & gas supermajors have all publicly recognized the need to address climate change.
- The Department of Defense has deemed climate change a threat to national security.
- It's time for action.

Chapter 2 – People and Property at Risk

I hate mosquitoes. On too many nights, I've been jolted awake by their infernal buzz. September 2014 was a particularly hot month in San Francisco. At the time, my bedroom was on the top floor of a three-story house. It had neither fans nor AC. On the hottest days, relief could only be found in open windows, the sunset breeze, and the other side of the pillow. September's hot weather proved ideal for mosquitoes; they arrived in swarms.

I can't remember being bitten a single time in the two years leading up to that month. I had never seen mosquitoes in San Francisco. The owners of the house had decades of experience living in this wonderful city, and they had no recollection of mosquitoes. Not surprisingly; after all, San Francisco is where winter spends the summer (at least, that used to be the case). September 2014 was—for me—a month of sleepless nights and endless itching. Those nights took their toll. I was genuinely tired, increasingly useless, and ill-tempered. Realizing there was no end in sight, I covered the windows with a new net. It was a necessary measure to address the sleep deficit and, perhaps, an early example of adaptation. Did I incur these costs because of climate change?

The science of attribution for individual events still has a long way to go. Nonetheless, this specific event provides insight into what life could be like in the Richmond District of San Francisco. It triggers an important mental exercise... that of thinking ahead about the unexpected consequences of rising temperatures. You may find my mosquito vignette amusing, but keep in mind that, while a mere nuisance for me, mosquitoes are a serious health threat around the world. Experts have been studying in great detail how vector populations (mosquitoes, ticks, fleas etc.) will be impacted by climate change. This is a priority concern, considering the diseases they can carry. Dr. Margaret Chan, acting Director General of the World

Health Organization, wrote in September 2014: "Many of the world's most worrisome diseases have transmission cycles that are profoundly shaped by conditions of heat and humidity and patterns of rainfall. As one important example, malaria parasites and the mosquitoes that transmit them are highly sensitive to climate variability, which has been repeatedly linked to epidemics … All of these diseases have a huge potential for social disruption and make huge logistical demands on response teams."[25]

What happened during September 2014 shaped my projections for how life might evolve in San Francisco. Before that dreadful month, I couldn't care less if a house in San Francisco had an AC unit, but—other things being equal—I now place greater value on houses with AC units. In fact, I visited several open houses the weekend before finishing this chapter and found myself looking for that friendly thermostat with light blue settings hanging on the wall. While an anomaly at present, I think it is probable that the presence of those annoying mosquitoes will become the norm in the future, and I expect to incur greater expenses to fight them off. Someday soon, I will probably succumb to buying an AC, hoping the cold air will keep the pests out of the bedroom!

Warmer temperatures are indeed in the cards for California. In assessing the regional economic impact of climate change, the educational platform Risky Business highlights increasing temperatures and its effects. The platform, already introduced in prior chapters, is a well-funded initiative co-chaired by prominent business leaders like former Secretary of the Treasury and Goldman Sachs CEO Hank Paulson, as well as former NYC Mayor and billionaire entrepreneur Michael Bloomberg. Its objectives are to study in detail the regional economic risks of climate change and to empower action by decision makers on a local level. When I interviewed Kate Gordon, former

[25] http://www.huffingtonpost.com/dr-margaret-chan/how-climate-change-can-ra_b_5822950.html

People and Property at Risk

Executive Director at Risky Business and now Vice Chair for Climate and Sustainable Urbanization at the Paulson Institute, she emphasized the critical importance of a local perspective. For Gordon, averages conceal the more dangerous extremes. As an example, the researchers at Risky Business found the decline in agricultural output averaged across the United States was moderate, but when looking at individual areas, the impacts were in some cases devastating. Missouri was expected to suffer "annual losses in corn yields of up to 24 percent over the next 5 to 25 years on average."[26] Without adaptation measures the losses are projected to increase throughout the century.

The summary report for the Southwest of the United States reads, "The Southwest will likely become hotter and more arid, increasing the intensity of wildfires, exacerbating drought, and increasing energy demand." The report forecasts the average number of days with temperatures above 95°C to grow by one to two months before the end of this century. The consequences of higher heat include lower labor productivity, higher energy expenditures, and, most concerning, higher mortality rates. The health dangers of hotter days are many, but remain poorly understood and neglected by most. I certainly didn't know that, for the last decade, heat was the leading cause of weather-related deaths in the United States. There are measurable spikes in hospital admissions and mortality rates during and following heat waves. In fact, the Centers for Disease and Prevention (CDC) actively studies how to prepare and respond to extreme heat events, stating: "Deaths and illnesses associated with extreme heat events will likely increase as more frequent, longer, and more severe future extreme heat events occur. There is a clear need for enhanced recognition of the public health challenges that future extreme heat events will pose."[27]

---

[26] http://riskybusiness.org/
[27] http://www.cdc.gov/climateandhealth/pubs/ClimateChangeandExtremeHeatEvents.pdf

People and Property at Risk

San Francisco is neither an exceptional situation nor the canary in the coal mine. In the recent documentary *Disruption* (2014), we hear, "All that we witness today is already in the context of an altered climate." Sometimes it's hard to perceive the changes because at their historic pace we just get used to them. It's like looking at a picture of ourselves from a few years ago. Often until that moment we don't realize how much we have changed. In an article called "Global Warming is Changing the Seasons," The Clear Path Foundation presented a clever quiz for readers where they asked simple questions like "Is Spring Blooming Earlier?" or "Is Winter Getting Colder?" They then showed the data for all 50 states and regions of the United States respectively.[28] The answer to the former question was yes and to the latter question a clear no. Compared to the first half of the 20th century, some regions have seen up to 19 fewer days of temperatures cold enough for snow! In summary, there is no shortage of examples of people having to adapt to the first impacts of climate change. Here are a few more:

Example 1: As mentioned, shorter winters and dryer summers are impacting the livelihoods of many mountain communities. Spring arrives in Lake Tahoe, for example, more than two weeks earlier than it did 50 years ago.[29] It is estimated the Northern Hemisphere has lost a million square miles of spring snowpack since 1970.[30] It is forecasted that the majority of major ski resorts in the United States will struggle to remain open by the end of this century. These communities are not only facing a threat to their economic vitality. In some instances, basic needs are at stake. Water shortages are now a growing risk for the summer months. The town of Aspen, for example, is considering building new reservoirs to secure enough supply for peak summer demand. Fully aware of

---

[28] http://www.clearpath.org/en/latest/more-featured-stories/global-warming-changing-the-seasons.html
[29] http://www.nytimes.com/2014/02/08/opinion/sunday/the-end-of-snow.html?_r=1
[30] http://protectourwinters.org/climate-science-and-solutions/

the threats of climate change to the region, community leaders in Aspen have been preparing as best they can. Not surprisingly, Aspen is now 100 percent powered by renewable energy!

Community leaders from many mountain towns and cities are coming together to address the threat of climate change, for there is strength in unity. Some of their efforts are focused on climate change mitigation, while others are geared towards improving local resilience. Not surprisingly, more than 100 ski areas have signed the CERES climate declaration, calling for meaningful policy action in the United States. The list includes Alta, Aspen Snowmass, Beaver Creek, Jackson Hole, Killington, Squaw Valley, Vail and Wintergreen, to name a few.

Other initiatives include Protect Our Winters (POW), where prominent athletes like professional snowboarder Jeremy Jones add their voices to the climate change movement. The Colorado chapter seeks to remind residents of what is at stake, roughly 12 million skier visits per year, supporting almost 40,000 jobs.[31] Not surprisingly, POW and similar initiatives are often backed by major sports brands like Patagonia, The North Face and Cliff Bars. Businesses are also taking a more active stance, sometimes the leading role. Auden Schendler, Vice President of Sustainability at Aspen Snowmass, is a great example; he has been hard at work for many years, educating the patrons of Snowmass on these issues. He pulls no punches in tackling this existential threat to the sports so many of us love.

Example 2: Perhaps the most well-known examples of communities vulnerable to climate change are those in low-lying coastal areas vulnerable to sea level rise. In some areas of the northeastern United States, sea levels are already a foot higher than early last century! For a long time, my understanding was that sea levels would rise

[31] http://protectourwinters.org/

nearer the end of the current century. I was wrong, as is illustrated by the following stories from various regions of the United States.

As mentioned in the previous chapter, the science team for the award-winning docuseries *Years of Living Dangerously* estimated that, during the course of 2012 Superstorm Sandy, the fact that sea levels were already one foot higher caused over 100,000 additional people across New York and New Jersey to be affected by the storm's devastating surge.

In Miami, Florida, salt water is contaminating fresh water supplies that were previously out of reach.[32] Flooding is now a recurrent hassle, particularly during the infamous autumn "king tides," when a combination of the season's warmer waters, a slower gulfstream current and the lunar cycle push the tide up to record levels. The city is fighting a race against time by investing millions of dollars in water pumps. In the last 20 years alone the sea level went up by four inches. Building sea walls is not an option for Miami; the city was built on porous limestone, allowing water to rise from below ground to the surface. Tide measurements show the rate of sea level rise in Miami is itself accelerating.[33] Risky Business estimates that across Florida between $5.6 billion and $14.8 billion dollars of coastal property will be lost by 2030.

Head west and the story is similar. Risky Business states that the most recent projection for sea level rise in San Diego is 0.7 to 1.2 feet by mid-century and 1.9 to 3.4 feet by the end of the century.[34] The main problem is tail risk; in other words, there are plausible scenarios where sea level rise is even greater. Up north in Alaska, entire villages like

---

[32] http://www.rollingstone.com/politics/news/why-the-city-of-miami-is-doomed-to-drown-20130620?page=2

[33] http://www.miaminewtimes.com/news/sea-level-rise-threatens-to-drown-miami-even-faster-than-feared-um-researcher-finds-6537603

[34] http://riskybusiness.org/site/assets/uploads/2015/09/California-Report-WEB-3-30-15.pdf

31

Kivalina, with a population of 400, need to be relocated. Sea level, coupled with melting permafrost, is accelerating the rate of coastal erosion. Up to a dozen communities have already been identified as at risk of relocation. Paradoxically, the state government might have difficulty coming up with the millions of dollars for relocation costs (per community) if current revenues from oil and gas exploration decline. Today, the state of Alaska finances almost its entire budget with levies on oil and gas production.[35]

Along the coastline, billions of dollars of property will be underwater in the coming decades. Are homebuyers and owners paying attention? Are the communities in which they are investing adequately preparing for the future? The US Army Corp of Engineers issued guidelines to its staff requiring all future projects to encompass sea level rise projections.[36] Unfortunately, not everyone is as prudent; it isn't difficult to find towns with outdated building codes or land use plans, even when the risks and potential effects are undeniable! The American Society of Civil Engineers also assembled a committee on Climate Change Adaptation, expecting it will lead to the establishment of new standards.[37] Its 2011 president, D. Wayne Klotz, was quoted by the *New York Times,* reminding people that "…municipal building codes that govern minimum standards for many structures often lag behind what is happening in the real world, because of the slow pace of lawmaking."[38]

Recurrent flooding is also a major concern for the Hamptons Roads, VA, area, home to the world's largest naval base. In 2015, sea levels were 14 inches higher than in 1930. The base is prepping for millions of dollars in renovations, a necessary measure to prevent flooding from

---

[35] http://www.bbc.com/news/science-environment-34501867

[36] http://www.corpsclimate.us/rcc.cfm

[37] http://www.asce.org/climate-change/committee-on-adaptation-to-a-changing-climate/

[38] http://www.nytimes.com/2011/02/13/weekinreview/13rosenthal.html

compromising mission readiness. A total of 14 piers will have to be renovated, at an estimated cost of $35M each.[39]

A challenge faced by the armed forces is that, with 90 percent of the staff living off base, an effective solution will require coordination with the surrounding communities. According to the Center for Sea Level Rise, located in nearby Norfolk, "... up to 877 miles of roads in and around Hampton Roads could be regularly or permanently flooded if sea levels rise 3 feet." Flooding is so problematic in Norfolk that Mayor Paul Fraim admitted in a filmed interview for PBS in 2012 that it might be the first town that will have to concede property back to the sea or—as he called it—"retreat."

Drive down certain streets of Norfolk and you will see houses raised several feet in the air. Sadly, next-door neighbors might not be so lucky. Some don't have the creditworthiness necessary to get a loan. Others wait near the bottom of a long list of applicants for FEMA grants to help pay for the cost of raising their houses, which have been categorized as "repetitive losses." The truly unlucky ones face astronomical flood insurance premiums (up in the thousands of dollars); they can't get a mortgage without it. I was saddened to see so many "for sale" signs when I last visited.

Not surprisingly, there are now initiatives like the Center for Sea Level Rise at Old Dominion University. The center brings together stakeholders from across the region—including the military, politicians from both sides of the aisle, academics, and business leaders—in a collaborative effort to address a common threat. According to the center, there are hundreds of miles of road and billions of dollars in property at risk.

In Louisiana, the situation is also dire. The effects of sea level rise are compounded by mismanagement of the

---

[39] http://www.centerforsealevelrise.org/

Mississippi River and careless dredging. Land loss is so profound that some places can now only be seen on old maps. About a football field of wetlands is lost every hour, according the US Geological Survey.[40] Proposed restoration plans have billion-dollar price tags, making them hard to fund.

To help people better visualize the risks, the National Oceanic and Atmospheric Agency (NOAA) has developed an interactive online map.[41] It allows users to see which broad areas are likely to be underwater for different amounts of sea level rise. It also overlays an analysis of social and economic risks based on an assessment of multiple indicators like population size, age and poverty. I encourage you to go online and, using the tool, zoom in on a coastal city. Raise the bar on the map to six feet and you'll see the shades of red taking over. Even my beloved Cambridge, MA, where I spent two of the best years of my life, takes a hit. I suspect over time the map will be perfected, offering more user-friendly graphics and granular forecasts. Regardless, I strongly recommend giving it a go if you haven't already. It really does put things into perspective.

In some of the most vulnerable areas, the topic is avoided for political reasons. The city of Norfolk is very active on climate change, but some of its neighbors in the Hampton Roads area facing the exact same situation have opted to almost completely disregard the issue. More disturbingly, there are instances of state senates prohibiting the use of climate change-related terminology in state bills (Virginia) or restricting the use of sea level rise forecasts for planning purposes (North Carolina). There is pressure, however, from many sources—ranging from local citizens to big businesses—to address issues related to sea level rise. At the forefront are the influential insurance companies

---

[40]http://www.nola.com/environment/index.ssf/2011/06/louisiana_is_losing_a_foot ball.html
[41] https://coast.noaa.gov/slr/

Munich Re, Swiss Re and Lloyds. The latter is the world's oldest continuously-operated insurance market. These companies have been very vocal in promoting action and active in the calibration of catastrophe models to appropriately factor in climate change. Munich Re estimated that global weather-related losses and damage increased from an average of $50bn per year in the 1980s to close to $200bn per year in the early 2000s.[42] Even with funding and insurance, a key concern is: What happens if worst-case scenarios for sea level rise pan out? At what point is it more logical to "retreat?" This is, by no means, a trivial question. The economics may be relatively straightforward, but when you are on the front line, there is much more at stake. Personal roots go deep.

Example 3: While conducting research for a documentary project on climate change, I traveled to Boulder, Colorado, to meet with scientists at one of NOAA's facility. During those meetings I asked each of them a simple question: had their knowledge of climate change been a determining factor in any recent major life decision?

One of the scientists replied he had sold his house up in the mountains to move closer to the city. Why? The hot summer of 2012 had been incredibly uncomfortable. Realizing that, according to studies by his peers, summer weather was representative of the future, he decided it was time to sell. This wasn't just about comfort; there were legitimate concerns of increasing wildfire risk. Fire seasons are substantially longer today, covering vast and growing swaths of land. Higher temperatures, more drought, and an increasing number of dead trees—all resulting from climate change—are creating ideal conditions for wildfires. Parts of the United States saw increases of 650 percent in the amount of area burned between 1970 and the early 2000s.[43] The trend continues.

---

[42] http://www.worldbank.org/en/news/feature/2013/11/18/disaster-climate-resilience-in-a-changing-world
[43] http://nca2014.globalchange.gov/highlights/regions/southwest

The scientist's answer immediately prompted two questions in mind. First, did the buyer have access to the same information when he/she agreed to the final price? Second, did the buyer have the knowledge required to reasonably interpret that information? Perhaps he/she did or perhaps not. Many areas of the United States follow the convention of "caveat emptor," or let the buyer beware. Risks like sea level rise-induced flooding or wildfires aren't mandatory disclosures for sellers. (Termite damage is an example of a mandatory disclosure in real estate sales.) While this is likely to change over time, many people will be caught unawares in the process.

In this chapter I've given you a mere taste of what is happening across the United States. If you are interested in learning more about the impacts in your particular region, I suggest you start online with the National Climate Assessment Highlights Report and the Risky Business Platform. I also encourage you to watch the docuseries *Years of Living Dangerously*.

Chapter takeaways:

- There is no shortage of climate change manifestations across the US.
- The impacts are undeniable and the stakes are very high.
- The ski industry and livelihood of mountain communities are at risk.
- Coastal towns are feeling the first impacts of sea level rise, with some residents actively contemplating retreating and/or relocating.
- The number and intensity of heat waves (a major health hazard, in particular, for the young and old) is increasing, as is the case with droughts and wildfires.
- Climate change is already influencing key decisions made by well-informed individuals, businesses, communities and organizations.

Chapter 3 - Finding Safe Harbor

In 2014, Standard & Poor's announced that climate change would be factored into their risk assessments of sovereign debt.[44] The logic was simple: if a country is likely to suffer from climate change and is inadequately prepared for the impacts, then it will likely face additional financial difficulties. Other things being equal, the country will find it harder to pay its debts. An important takeaway from this announcement is that investors and their advisors are factoring climate change into their decisions. They know that some communities are more exposed and less prepared for the impacts of climate change than others. As a result, they are devoting time and money to figuring out what climate change means for their investment portfolios.

The CERES Investor Network on Climate Risk (INCR) represents trillions of dollars in assets and includes prominent institutions like BlackRock, CalPERS, KKR and Rockefeller Financial in its member base. The network actively exerts pressure on companies for better disclosure of climate risks through, among other means, petitions to regulators (such as the Securities and Exchange Commission) seeking more formal and stringent disclosure requirements. These efforts are paying off. In 2010, the SEC released its Commission Guidance Regarding Disclosure Related to Climate Change.

The release reminded companies not to ignore climate change because, technically, it already falls within the parameters of existing disclosure requirements. All companies are obliged to identify material risks related to regulatory change (including environmental laws), physical events (for example, extreme weather), and indirect risks (such as changes in the cost of raw materials as a result of the prior two).

---

[44] http://www.bloomberg.com/news/articles/2014-05-15/climate-change-to-hit-sovereign-creditworthiness-s-p

The number of companies opting to get involved is growing. Several are starting to take a more proactive and—truth be told—prudent stance in preparing for the changes ahead. Coca Cola and Nike, for example, have started to analyze what climate change means for their strategies and operations.[45] They want to know how their supply chains might be impacted and what steps they should be taking to improve their resilience. These efforts have already resulted in changes to existing practices. Nike is reportedly using more synthetic materials, in part because their supply is less conditional on the weather. Coca Cola is applying water conservation technologies for the very same reason.

These actions are examples of prudent risk management, arguably falling within the basic tenets of fiduciary duty. The risks are real. In 2011, for example, floods in Thailand disrupted the global supply chain for hard drives. Multiple assembly lines were concentrated in the same geographic area, which was battered by heavy rains during an unusually strong monsoon season. As a result, computer manufacturers experienced a material decline in revenues, with the global giant Acer reportedly lowering its fourth quarter sales projection by 5 to 10 percent.[46]

When figuring out what to do, advice is sought from research organizations like the Notre Dame Global Adaptation Index (ND-GAIN), which analyzes climate change risks on a country level. Examining a broad range of indicators, the team at Notre Dame determines which countries are vulnerable as well as their readiness to address those vulnerabilities. Not surprisingly, risk is higher in less-developed economies; many African countries rank poorly.[47] It is a well-known fact that the more marginalized members of society are most impacted

---

[45] http://www.nytimes.com/2014/01/24/science/earth/threat-to-bottom-line-spurs-action-on-climate.html

[46] https://www.pwc.com/us/en/corporate-sustainability-climate-change/assets/pwc-sustaining-the-supply-chain-july-2012.pdf

[47] http://www.gain.org/

by climate change. They are the least likely, for example, to be able to absorb food price increases from declining crop yields. The World Food Programme estimates that without action to increase climate resilience around the world, the risk of hunger and malnutrition will increase by up to 20 percent before 2050![48] In January 2015, the Notre Dame Adaptation Index project received funding from the Kresge Foundation to further develop their assessment of the United States. The purpose of the grant was to enable a more granular study of different U.S. cities. The Foundation hopes to help people in these cities make better decisions with the information provided. The Foundation supports "efforts that are anchored in cities" because the requirements for improving our resilience to climate change are essentially local.[49] The problems faced by coastal cities vary significantly from those faced by their rural compatriots. Measures to increase resilience need to be tailored to idiosyncrasies of each location, not just in terms of climate patterns, but also in terms of the built environment, laws (zoning, building codes…) and the level of social and political stability.

As you will have noticed by now, this is one of many efforts to study and communicate the reality of climate change. When it comes to this topic, there continues to be a big mismatch between public opinion and expert knowledge. I cannot reiterate this point enough. When scientists, the military, investors, executives, and civic leaders are paying this much attention, shouldn't you? Buying a home is the biggest expenditure most people will undertake in their lives, and I'm concerned that very few think about climate change when they do so. A corollary of this statement is that most people are making incomplete appraisals of property values when buying a home. I sincerely hope these examples convince you to be more considerate of climate change when you next pick a community in which

---

[48] https://www.wfp.org/climate-change
[49] http://kresge.org/programs/environment

to live and build your home. It can be what makes the difference in your quest for safe harbor.

In order to make a more informed decision, start by asking the following 4 questions:
1. What are the risks to the area?
2. How prepared is the community?
3. Can you tolerate the identified risks?
4. Do property prices adequately reflect the risks?

1. What are the risks to the area?

You can conduct this basic assessment on multiple levels - from countries to individual properties. One approach is to start at a higher level and proceed to narrow your option set. For most of us, this set is narrow to begin with, as few people can easily relocate to another country.

As an example, this book focuses on changes at the level of the community and surrounding region. The starting point is a list of standard risks associated with climate change. Using the results of the *National Climate Assessment* and similar resources, we can compile a simple list of first-order and second-order effects:

- First-order effects: Extreme heat, heavy downpours, intense storms, drought, flooding and sea level rise
- Second-order effects: Water shortages, food shortages, wildfires, deteriorating health (heat, air quality, vector-carried diseases, etc.), productivity declines, and compromised infrastructure (energy, transportation, emergency response and other civil services, etc.)

With this list as a starting point, you can think about which of these applies to the area you are considering. Some of the risks, like sea level rise in low-lying coastal communities, are more obvious than others, like drought. California, for example, has experienced intense drought for a number of years, but the state's residents are not equally burdened. Water keeps flowing from faucets in San Francisco. The city's dwellers are less likely to think about the drought and its implications than farmers in the Central Valley.

Some risks require even more research, partly because of an inconsistency in weather patterns. Don't forget that you may be exploring the area in a good year! Natural weather cycles can temporarily mask the evolution of the baseline. A powerful and well-known example is, of course, El Nino, which occurs every three to seven years. During a strong El Nino year, weaker winds over the Pacific Ocean prevent warm surface waters from being pushed from the Americas toward Asia. The resulting spread of warm water across the Pacific has a dramatic impact on US weather. 1998 was a very strong El Nino year,[50] causing billions of dollars in damages from floods for traditionally drought-prone states like California and Texas.

Having conversations with long-term residents and doing some online research will help you get a more representative and informative data set. You should be on the lookout for past extreme weather events to see if there are any patterns. This will enable you to discern which climate-related disruptions a region is more prone to experience. A variety of online tools allows you to find weather events for a region; among them is the NOAA Climatic Data Center website. This website gives you access to resources like the Storm Events Database, which tracks data on all sorts of extreme events, from astronomical low tides to dust devils. Using it, you can pick any county in the United States, like Cook County in Illinois, and generate a list of what's happened there since, for example, the year 2000. The database provides you with a summary table for your search and a line item record for each major event. You can even sort the results using different filters, such as the number of deaths, and

---

[50] http://www.clearpath.org/en/latest/more-featured-stories/curious-case-of-el-nino.html

find that heat is repeatedly the number one killer in Chicago. Twenty-three people died of excessive heat in July 2012.[51]

Next, you need to consider potential domino or knock-on effects, the third- and fourth- order effects. For example, if a key pillar of the local economy is experiencing rapid change, then what does that mean for the town's livelihood? Subsequently, what would that mean for your own livelihood?

In New England, fisheries are dealing with declining populations of commercially important species such as shrimp and lobster.[52] Rising ocean temperatures are believed to be the main culprit. Consequently, former Republican Senator Olympia J. Snowe has become a vocal advocate for action on climate change, which is particularly laudable given the party politics of climate change in the United States today. Her actions are driven by the need to protect historic pillars of Maine's economy, as well as the people and communities whose livelihoods are at stake.

In many instances, climate change is like steroids for existing challenges. If you already have a weak immune system, you are probably more vulnerable to heat-induced stress. Now apply this logic to the case of an impoverished nation: if a country already suffers from food shortages or political instability, disruptions caused by more frequent and volatile weather extremes will only make matters worse. What will happen in these instances? Are communities capable of withstanding the shock? If not, you should be aware of this before you decide to live in such places. Otherwise, you risk building your home in an area prone to suffering a terrible vicious cycle. The lack of social cohesion and a robust infrastructure enables climate

---

[51] http://www.ncdc.noaa.gov/stormevents/
[52] http://www.newsweek.com/lack-action-climate-change-costing-fishing-jobs-305642

change to be more destructive than it would otherwise be. That destruction then further erodes social cohesion and tears away the infrastructure required to effectively respond to climate change, for example, an exodus can occur in the aftermath of a big storm or severe drought.

In the episode "Climate Wars" of the docuseries *Years of Living Dangerously*, Thomas Friedman explores how climate change may already have been a key determinant of recent conflicts. For example, before deadly civil war erupted in Syria, its people suffered an extreme multi-year drought. Egypt, the world's biggest wheat importer, experienced rapid inflation in bread prices in the run-up to Egypt's Arab Spring revolution.[53] In Tahrir Square, Egyptians chanted, "Bread, freedom and dignity!" Global wheat prices were soaring due to weather disruptions. Shortly before that revolution, for example, a heat wave in Russia crippled the country's output and led to an export moratorium.[54]

By now, you will have realized that there are ample risks to consider but, fortunately, not all will be relevant when you are looking at a specific community. For those that are relevant, the next step is to determine how impactful they can be. This depends on the answer to our second question, which focuses on the resilience of a community's physical and social infrastructure.

2. How prepared is this community?
To answer this question, there are four key elements to consider. The first element is the extent to which the community is being proactive, starting with visible and substantive efforts to study the effects of climate change. Is there a robust, ongoing effort or a clear attention deficit? If information is hard to find, that should be an automatic red flag. In contrast, proactive measures include the

[53] http://www.theguardian.com/lifeandstyle/2011/jul/17/bread-food-arab-spring
[54] http://www.nytimes.com/2015/09/09/opinion/extreme-weather-and-food-shocks.html?_r=0

commissioning of dedicated studies, the nomination of an official point person, dedicated team or committee, and/or the establishment of a permanent office. In 2013, for example, the governor of Colorado created the position of a Climate Change Czar in the state's Energy Office.[55] Cities and towns across the United States have created comparable positions at their scale.

The city of Aspen's Canary Initiative was established to manage both mitigation and resilience efforts. The work involves proposing and developing goals with different stakeholders. Once these goals are approved by the city council, the Initiative helps manage implementation and track progress. In 2015, the town's goals included reducing their own emissions 30 percent by 2020 and 80 percent by 2050, relative to a 2004 baseline.[56] The Initiative's studies focus on the issues that are most relevant to Aspen, a list that includes temperature trends, changes in precipitation patterns, the number of frost-free days, and the migration of plant and animal species across elevations, which are a direct result of the above. They then look at knock-on effects and the impacts on the area's intrinsic risks like wildfires, flooding and landslides. Their work includes outreach efforts ranging from interviews with individual community members to town hall meetings.

These efforts serve the dual purpose of collecting information from Aspen's residents and of better informing residents and property owners. When applicable, the outreach efforts serve to encourage the adoption of proven resilience measures at the individual property level. As stated in one of their reports, existing infrastructure was built assuming outdated variations in the climate. The report cites one problem in particular that is becoming familiar to many people across the United States as temperatures rise: "Many Aspen buildings [are] only

---

[55] http://www.denverpost.com/news/ci_23354097/colo-getting-climate-change-czar

[56] http://aspenpitkin.com/Living-in-the-Valley/Green-Initiatives/Canary-Initiative/

equipped with heating systems, more days per year with high temperatures above tolerable comfort zones could involve significant capital investment to install cooling systems through retrofit."

Another example involves the previously mentioned Center for Sea Level Rise in the Hampton Roads area. Interestingly, the Center started by focusing largely on the symptom—sea level rise—thereby avoiding giving excessive attention to the underlying cause: climate change. The reason for this approach was the unfortunate politicization of climate change in the United States. It was determined that focusing on sea level rise alone would attract a larger set of regional stakeholders and avoid unproductive confrontations. As one community leader, Skip Stiles Wetlands Watch Executive Director, told me, "First, I have to get people on the bus."

In your research, you may find locations where laws and practices are grossly outdated, sometimes even encouraging risky behavior. Flood insurance is a prime example. Insurance rates are usually driven by the classification of zones based on their chances of flooding. In many areas, zones will not have been updated for a long time, meaning insurance rates are lower than they should be, and people feel safer living there than they should. Building codes that ignore climate projections is another example. Urban spaces subject to "heat island effects" is yet another. In the UK, for example, the resilience to extreme weather report, released in 2014 by the Royal Society, criticized continued population growth in increasingly at-risk areas. It highlighted the need for greater government intervention in order to ensure more resilient societies.[57]

As time progresses, however, you will likely be able to consult centralized sources of information with standardized ways of assessing climate-related risks. I

---

[57] https://royalsociety.org/policy/projects/resilience-extreme-weather/

have mentioned several examples of projects working towards making more detailed local assessments available. These include Risky Business, the Notre Dame GAIN index, and NOAA's interactive sea level rise viewer. Other initiatives are also underway. Some specialize in particular fields, like The Nature Conservancy's Coastal Resilience tool, which is more focused on the use of nature-based solutions for sea level rise.

Emerging crowd-sourced platforms are also keeping up with evolving technology and cultural norms. For example, iseechange.org encourages people to submit noticeable deviations in local weather patterns that may be attributable to climate change. It matches the submitted events with data from NASA satellites and looks for corroborating posts from other members of that community. Scientists are then brought in to study what is being flagged on the ground.

In the near future, these types of studies are likely to become common practice for states, if not simply mandatory. The Federal Emergency Management Agency (FEMA) issued new guidelines, expected to take effect in 2016, stating that access to disaster preparedness funds (which are different from disaster response funds) would be conditional on the states studying the threats posed by climate change.[58]

The second element to consider when assessing a community's commitment to addressing climate change is the extent to which an adequate response plan has been formulated and, if necessary, implemented. In New York City, former Mayor Bloomberg launched the ongoing PlaNYC, the city's "sustainability and resiliency blueprint." It started with an in-depth examination of how the city will be impacted by climate change. Based on the findings, detailed plans were developed, many of which have

---

[58] http://www.washingtontimes.com/news/2015/mar/23/fema-rules-trouble-for-climate-change-deniers/

already been put in place.[59] The broad set of measures includes:

- Working with communities to improve zoning laws
- Rewriting building laws to factor in sea level rise
- Strengthening infrastructure by partnering with service providers (like electric utilities) to take into account low-probability, high-impact events
- Working with communities to ensure adequate insurance coverage and helping them cope with pending federal insurance reform
- Planting trees and applying reflective surfaces to rooftops in order to mitigate the urban heat island effect (by 2014, six million square feet had already been coated with reflective paint)
- Implementing short-term measures to reduce immediate risks, such as placing additional sand on city beaches
- Committing to an 80 percent reduction in emissions by 2050, as did Aspen and New York City (with its impressive population of eight million people)

San Diego's Climate Collaborative is a network of public agencies working together and in partnership with academic institutions, businesses and nonprofits to develop a comprehensive response to climate change. Among the resilience measures being adopted in San Diego, in light of California's history of drought, are impressive water conservation efforts.

These examples are likely to become the norm. In fact, network-type initiatives now span countries and continents. They include ICLEI—local governments for sustainability, the C40 group—a network of the world's megacities committed to addressing climate change, and the Rockefeller Foundation's 100 Resilient Cities Program. The benefits of these initiatives include knowledge and best practice sharing; I suspect they will also lead to greater solidarity among participants as events unfold. The

---

[59] http://www.nyc.gov/html/planyc/html/home/home.shtml

100 Resilient City Program is creating a partner network and pooling cross-disciplinary teams. These include emerging tech industry startups like Palantir, which is helping derive big-data solutions useful for things like the management of emergency services.

The third element to consider is: What does history teach you about the community's resilience to shocks? For example, what happened the last time there was a flood? Was there an assessment of what went well and what needed improvement? Did that assessment produce actionable recommendations? Were those recommendations implemented in a timely manner?

The fourth and final element to look for is leadership. Community leaders can enable or they can hinder progress. Some leaders have publicly stated that they simply do not believe in climate change. It is unlikely, in those circumstances, that they would devote any resources to addressing this challenge.

An extreme example occurred when Senator Jim Inhofe, a well-known skeptic of the reality of climate change, threw a snowball on the Senate floor as if he were presenting irrefutable and tangible evidence that global warming was a hoax. What makes the example even more discouraging is that the senator was, at the time, chairman of the U.S. Senate Committee on Environment in Public Works, which is responsible for oversight of federal agencies like NOAA.

The Florida Center for Investigative Reporting reported that state officials were actively discouraged from talking or writing about climate following an "unwritten ban" supposedly originating in the office of Governor Rick Scott.[60] When questioned publicly, officials denied the claims, but—sadly—there continue to be many cases across the US where public officials actively deny–or try to avoid—the topic of climate change. The latter is just as bad as the

---

[60] http://www.miamiherald.com/news/local/environment/article15409031.html

49

former if the end result is a mitigation and resilience deficit. Sometimes denial is not political, but stems from fear and the way our brains work. Psychologists have noted that, as a species, we like both confidence and conformity. One expert at NOAA suggested that some communities avoid the topic because "... if you talk about it, you are seen as vulnerable." I've witnessed this myself when doing researching for my documentary; one realtor whom I interviewed acknowledged that he was concerned that talking about climate change might lead to alarmism, depriving his town of needed investment.

Marshall Saunders, founder of Citizens Climate Lobby, reminded me of the emblematic scene in Spielberg's classic movie *Jaws*. The first shark attacks are discussed at a town meeting where the dominant voices ensure the issue is kept quiet. They don't want panic that could scare away tourists and hurt their businesses. An interesting study on these types of dynamics is the book I mentioned earlier, *Don't Even Think About It: Why Our Brains Are Wired to Ignore Climate Change*, by George Marshall. Using a rich set of examples, Marshall describes the various reasons all of us (myself included) hesitate so much to acknowledge and act on the difficult reality of climate change. We do so despite the fact it is to our own detriment. It is never sensible to ignore a problem simply because its implications are hard to swallow. Inaction can quickly lead to a manageable situation becoming a disaster. Even leaders who do care about climate may, however, not have the right incentives or may simply lack the bandwidth to do anything about it. Their priorities might be determined by other needs competing for attention. Time in office for many elected officials is capped and election cycles are short relative to the impacts of decisions (or lack of) on climate change.

During international negotiations on climate change, some participants have argued that cutting GHG emissions should not be required of developing economies. They contend that we should, instead, wait for their economies to grow so they can muster the resources required to invest in resilience and mitigation. The logic, overly simplified for the purpose of illustration, is that only a rich nation can afford to tackle climate change, which is a secondary priority, at best, for malnourished people (don't ask people to pay for upgrading to clean energy when they can barely afford to eat). My personal view is that, while the logic of this argument makes sense, its underlying assumption is wrong. Believing fossil fuel-based economic growth will happen fast enough to leave time to address climate change is, in my view, wishful thinking, especially when we consider how difficult it actually is to achieve accelerated and lasting economic growth under normal circumstances.

In summary, to prioritize the short-term benefits of a particular planning model is a mistake. If climate change is not a priority on the agenda of local leaders, you have a major red flag.

3. Can you personally tolerate identified risks?

Having identified and measured the risks to the extent you can, it's time to decide whether this is a community you want to join. Answering this question requires determining your own vulnerability during high-impact, low-probability events... in other words, worst-case scenarios. Consider the following examples:

Example 1: The weather forecast for your town may include a trend towards more frequent heat waves, but you feel that, with air conditioning, your family can cope with it. The local economy is service-based, so it is unlikely the heat will alter the course of business. Droughts occur more often and last longer, but you bought your own water storage system. Consequently, service cuts for rationing purposes (such as those that happened in Sao Paulo, Brazil) won't impact you.[61] Furthermore, living in a city

---

[61] http://www.latimes.com/world/brazil/la-fg-brazil-drought-20150820-story.html

means you are not within reach of raging wildfires. In this example, you may opt to stay put.

Example 2: Intense storms are becoming more frequent, but your house is solid, and you are satisfied with emergency response services in the area and their surge capacity. Flooding might be more common but, unlike your neighbors, your house is raised above the 100-year floodplain, meaning insurance premiums are still affordable. In addition, the county is investing in flood defenses and raising your entire street. The height was based on the latest sea level rise projections. All of this is reassuring.

Example 3: Most people in your already economically-distressed community are on the edge. You don't believe the social fabric could withstand a shock to the system, and you would rather not expose your family to any ensuing security threats. In this case, a quick scan of likely climate change impacts might convince you to pack up and go.

In your assessment, don't forget there are unknowns. The complexity of our climate means surprises are in store. Drought conditions and shorter winters resulted in the unexpected death of millions of trees across North America, decimated by tiny bark beetles. Unlike sea level rise, we didn't see that one coming. The beetles have, thus far, killed more trees than all wildfires occurring during the same period put together![62] Consequently, you will be better off if you develop a habit for staying informed so that you can adjust your assessment as we develop our knowledge of climate change impacts.

Once you've developed these scenarios for the communities in which you are interested, you are in a much better position to make an informed decision about staying, leaving or joining a community. Keep in mind,

---

[62] http://yearsoflivingdangerously.com/topic/heat/

though, there isn't a community out there that won't experience climate change. There is no real safe harbor in the sense of being able to conserve the climate exactly as it has been. The manifestation and relative intensity of the changes is what will vary from place to place. In other words, you can be relatively safer and more protected from a certain set of changes in some areas, but never from all. If we consider how complex the climate really is, and how difficult it is for us to accurately predict the changes, we start to build a very strong case in favor of climate change mitigation, a topic discussed in detail in the last chapters.

4. Do property prices adequately reflect your prognostic?

The final step of this assessment concerns determining fair value. Consider the analogous example of stock prices. In recent years, several articles and studies have suggested that the stock prices of some fossil fuel companies are inconsistent with the politically-stated objective of limiting global warming to an average of 2 degrees Celsius. They claim that stock prices reflect a level of extraction of fossil fuel reserves that surpasses the limit corresponding to 2 degrees. In essence, they claim those stock prices are too high. The International Energy Agency has published reports warning about the risk of stranded assets (investments made by fossil fuel firms that cannot be recovered).[63] Pressure is mounting on these firms to (a) assess the risk of declining future demand for their products in light of mitigation efforts and (b) publicly reveal their findings. One non-profit group asking for this type of information is the Carbon Disclosure Project, which represents hundreds of institutional investors.

A recent study from University College London, *The Geographic Distribution of Fossil Fuels Unused When Limiting Global Warming to 2°C,* attempted to offer more precise estimates of what can and can't be used. By their estimate, 82 percent of the world's coal reserves, 49

---

[63] http://www.iea.org/publications/freepublications/publication/WEIO2014.pdf

percent of the world's gas reserves and 33 percent of the world's oil reserves would have to stay in the ground. Yet most fossil fuel companies continue to invest in exploration in order to further increase their reserves. There are several possible explanations for what is happening. For example, market participants could be putting their faith in emerging technologies—such as geo-engineering or carbon capture and storage—that would make it possible to address climate change while continuing to use fossil fuels. Unfortunately, these technologies are not commercially viable at present. In some cases a lot of groundwork is still required just in terms of basic research.

My personal view is that many investors remain ignorant of the significance and implications of climate change. As discussed earlier on, recent surveys demonstrate there continues to be a massive gap between public and expert opinion. Over time, this gap will close, as the changes in the climate become so pronounced they will be impossible to ignore. In the meantime, prices will adjust or, as one journalist said, "… finance will eventually have to surrender to physics."[64]

It may also be that market participants are playing "hot potato" with fossil fuel stocks. In this scenario, they may be fully aware that not all reserves will be extracted, but while they don't want to be left holding the stock when the markets adjust, they think they can make money now. We have seen this type of behavior in financial markets before. In market bubbles, such as the subprime bubble, market participants can behave like a herd moving in contradiction to the fundamental drivers of value. In June 2014, Hank Paulson, former Goldman Sachs CEO and Secretary of the Treasury under President George W. Bush, wrote an op-ed for the *New York Times* entitled "The Coming Climate Crash." In it, he stated, "Each of us must recognize that the risks are personal. We've seen and felt the costs of

---

[64] http://www.theguardian.com/environment/2015/mar/16/argument-divesting-fossil-fuels-overwhelming-climate-change

underestimating the financial bubble. Let's not ignore the climate bubble."

There is currently a globally-coordinated divestment movement encouraging investors to sell their assets in fossil fuel companies. It continues to grow as prominent investors, including the Rockefeller Brothers Fund and the Stanford University Endowment Fund, answer the call.[65] Market prices may adjust quickly and abruptly, or they may do so gradually over the years. Even very wily investors are playing a game of chicken at this point. Regardless, while public opinion remains divided about climate change, there are likely to be situations of asymmetric information and the party that is most knowledgeable may be able to profit from it.

For example, a healthy environment for snow sports ultimately determines property values at a ski resort. Assuming a declining number of days those sports can be enjoyed (due to temperature rise) and an accelerating rate of decline, a potential buyer must question the wisdom of investing in resort property. How will expectations of future demand influence today's ski lodge and residential property prices? Hypothetical buyers bought property on the mountain, planning to sell it in thirty years. The couple hoped the resort would not only bring them thirty years of fun skiing, but would be a great investment for their retirement. The value of property in the area had only appreciated since the resort was first created. Years later, they become aware of climate change and have noticed that the mountain's ski season is getting shorter. Property prices in the area continue to increase, however. So what should they do? Should they sell earlier than planned? If they do, should they be honest with the buyer about why? This example is hypothetical, but situations like these are certain to become common. In areas like Miami, where people are suffering from the more tangible issue of sea

---

[65] http://gofossilfree.org/

level rise, concerns about rising flood insurance premiums may eventually trigger broad price adjustments.[66]

Earlier in the book, disclosure laws were discussed. Not every state has stringent disclosure laws to protect buyers; many still follow "caveat emptor," or "let the buyer beware." Furthermore, because climate change is relatively new and incremental, it may take years before disclosure laws are rewritten to adequately reflect the risks of climate change and the associated costs.

A breakdown of climate change costs you may experience where you live includes:
- Implementation of resilience/adaptation measures on your properties
- Higher property maintenance costs
- Higher insurance premiums
- Increased taxes to pay for community infrastructure upgrades like new drainage systems or additional staff to cope with peak surge demand for emergency services
- Higher healthcare costs due to higher incidence rates like heat stress
- Higher food and water costs due to supply chain disruptions
- Higher energy costs due to heat induced efficiency losses (both for electricity transmission and generation equipment), greater usage of expensive "peak load" plants during demand surges on very hot days, damage to the grid from more natural disasters (storms, floods, wildfires...) and all the ensuing infrastructure upgrades and increased maintenance costs.

I cannot tell you which areas today are mispriced. What I can tell you is that a large number of prospective buyers and sellers are not well-informed about the impacts of

---

[66] http://ngm.nationalgeographic.com/2015/02/climate-change-economics/parker-text

climate change. The important thing is for you not to be one of them... for you not to be caught unawares. For major long-term decisions, like buying a house, the time has come for us to be as diligent as institutional investors when picking assets in which to invest. In fact, we should be even more diligent than institutional investors! After all, when we buy a house, a large share of our personal wealth is concentrated in that one property... sometimes an entire life's work. Investors have the luxury of being able to spread their investment portfolios across multiple asset classes—and multiple securities within each asset class—to hedge the risk of a few of them failing. They are trained to diversify... never to hold a large share of their portfolio in one stock or industry. The vast majority of us don't have that luxury, so let's pick wisely.

The simple act of asking the four questions outlined in this chapter will enable you to start developing an informed perspective: what are the risks, how prepared is the community, how prepared will you be, and do housing prices reflect the costs of climate change. Basically, think of the weather before moving in. Eventually, each of us will choose a community. Some people will have a strong inclination to stay where they are; it is home, and it has always been home. Regardless of how rational or emotional the choice, once you pick a place to stay, it's time to start preparing for when climate change hits home. That is the focus of the next chapter—how to fortify "home."

Chapter takeaways:

- Leading institutional investors and regulators are actively advocating for more stringent disclosures of climate change risks by publicly-traded companies.
- Climate change impacts are inherently local; resilience studies must be, too.
- Look at data for more than one year, since weather cycles can mask climate trends.
- To make an informed decision about where to live, analyze the likely risks of climate change to the area, the preparedness of the community to address those risks, your personal tolerance to the identified risks, and to what extent those risks are reflected in property prices.
- Be on the lookout for constraints, such as inadequate funding, uninformed policies, and outdated laws.
- Litmus tests should include the propensity for local leaders to talk about climate change, and the existence of regional adaptation and mitigation plans.
- Some cities, like NYC, are far ahead of the pack with initiatives like PlaNYC.
- Given the generally low level of basic awareness, it is extremely likely that asset prices (in particular, home prices) do not reflect climate change costs.

Chapter 4 – Fortifying Home

After deciding in which community to live, the question becomes... which property should I choose? At this point, your choices can still greatly influence your vulnerability to climate change. In fact, there might be a larger set of measures under your control; you should value the things that lower your exposure to the negative consequences of climate change.

Resilience measures should reflect the anticipated effects of climate change. Your starting point is the list of risks identified for your area, combined with an assessment of the frequency and impact of occurrences. These risks encompass impacts on personal health (such as heat stress), impacts on personal finances (including higher energy costs), and catastrophic impacts (like floods). My mosquito story illustrates this point well: if mosquitoes are going to become a fact of life during the summer months, and summer is going to last longer, then I will be better off if I stick to properties with mosquito screens (all other things being equal). More generally, if my community is going to be exposed to temperature extremes, then I will value properly insulated properties with effective heating and cooling systems. I will be on the lookout for things like air sealing, attic insulation, programmable thermostats and double-pane windows. As a starting point, I may hire an experienced contractor to conduct a comprehensive "energy audit," assessing the need and viability of adding these and similar features to my home.

If a community is subject to flooding, you should seek higher elevations and stay out of natural waterways. If higher elevations are not possible, you should seek out the houses that have been sufficiently raised. Otherwise, you may find yourself paying a substantial insurance premium or footing the bill for raising the house in the future. If a community is subject to extreme heat, you might prefer neighborhoods with green spaces and houses with lighter-colored roofs or "green" roofs (those with vegetation). If you plan on living in an area that is historically prone to social instability, then you would prefer properties in safer neighborhoods with enhanced security. If properties lack any of these increasingly desirable or required attributes, then you need to account for the costs of future retrofits when determining how much you can afford to pay. None of this new! Prospective buyers and sellers do this kind of problem-solving all the time. The difference is a change in the set of issues you are thinking about, some of which other market participants may be ignoring... at their peril.

Once again, there are first-, second-, and multiple-order effects to consider. To prepare for the possibility of wildfires in the countryside, you might clear trees near your dwelling, incorporate non-flammable building materials, establish escape routes, and verify the nearest location of fire respondents. Additionally, wildfires could be expected to disrupt power lines, causing power outages in your area, a second-order effect. In this case, you would prefer communities and homes with distributed generation and backup power capabilities, such as batteries and solar panels. Imagine a time when power disruptions—due to wildfires, storms, or droughts—become so common that utilities need to make substantial investments in their generation and transmission infrastructure. These investments would result in higher electricity prices, a third-order effect. In this scenario, your appreciation for energy efficient properties and distributed generation assets would have been worthwhile.

Today, there are many organizations helping people and businesses improve their energy efficiency. Energy.gov, for example, has an Energy-Saver section created as a guide for homeowners. Similar initiatives exist at the state and local level (Mass Save in Massachusetts and Retrofit Chicago in Chicago). The same is true for other countries. In the UK, for example, there is the non-profit Energy Saving Trust that does similar work. To this end, the Rocky

Mountain Institute launched their Residential Energy+ Initiative. The heart of the matter is the lack of transparency around energy performance when it comes to houses and buildings. Houses don't have an equivalent to the MPG metric we apply to cars. The institute believes that introducing this information in a standardized manner will enable a faster adoption of much-needed energy efficiency upgrades by homeowners.[67]

With these examples in mind, you are now better positioned to choose wisely. There is a wide set of actions you can take to increase your resilience. Some actions are dependent on where you live, while others are applicable to almost everyone. This book is not intended to be a comprehensive guide, but it should point you in the right direction. Our understanding of the issues and how to prepare continues to improve daily, so you will benefit greatly from staying informed because things WILL change. Before you adopt any measures, you need to research which are the most cost-effective. You should consider the fact that some measures might be too little, too late. If a certain amount of sea level rise is now unavoidable, for example, then perhaps it is time to cut your losses and not throw good money after bad. Do you really expect FEMA to use taxpayer dollars to subsidize the raising of every house at risk along the coastlines? Do you expect county taxes to keep being used to raise all the streets on which these homes were built? At one point, the Risky Business educational platform stated that new homeowners in certain areas might find their houses underwater before their 30-year mortgage is paid off. In addition, many homeowners today made decisions to buy homes based on outdated flood insurance premiums. They are struggling with adjusted premiums based on updated assessments of risk. I suspect this will become more common in the near future.

---

[67]http://blog.rmi.org/blog_2015_10_14_residential_energy_plus_and_transparenc y_making_value_visible_for_home_energy_performance

To summarize, here is a non-comprehensive list of common examples for different situations:

- If you expect more intense storms, consider installing window protection, ensuring proper drainage, and designing roofs for heavy downpours and houses that minimize wind load.
- If you expect warmer temperatures, consider improving general insulation, installing air conditioning, painting your roof a lighter color, or building a green roof.
- If you expect flooding, consider raising your house or having a first floor dedicated to non-livable areas.
- If you expect fires, consider investing in non-flammable materials, clearing vegetation around your house, and/or installing sprinkler systems.
- For all of these and others you may want to analyze your insurance policies and ensure you have adequate coverage.

Recognize that you are not alone in preparing for the future. The US federal government, for example, has ongoing initiatives across multiple agencies, some of which are listed on the EPA's website.[68] Among them is the Department of Defense, which stated in the 2014 Quadrennial Defense Review that it was undertaking a comprehensive assessment of climate change impacts on each of its thousands of installations worldwide.[69] When I interviewed Joe Bouchard, former commander of Naval Station Norfolk and later a fellow at the Blue Moon Fund Foundation working on climate change adaptation and security, he emphasized how military bases are not self-sufficient and frequently rely on community infrastructure for common needs like power, water, telecommunications and transportation to and from the base. He stated that on account of recent experience the military was growing wary of investing in bases where the surrounding community

---

[68] http://www.epa.gov/climatechange/impacts-adaptation/fed-programs.html
[69] http://www.defense.gov/pubs/2014_Quadrennial_Defense_Review.pdf

was, by ignoring climate change, putting military assets at risk.

Always keep in mind that your personal resilience to climate change is influenced by your community's resilience to climate change. Unfortunately, not every community leader is as diligent as the US military. So be careful about completely delegating your resilience or blindly consulting local authorities; they may have done less research on the matter than you have! But, you can have a positive influence on your community's preparedness. At heart, this is about engaging other members of your community, especially civic leaders and elected officials. Reach out to your elected officials and let them know that you want them to prepare your community for when climate change hits home. The US government makes it easy to reach out to them, providing contact information for everyone from county officials and mayors to senators and the White House. Just visit the government website on How to Contact Elected Officials.[70]

There is indeed a long list of resources that you can share with them. Multiple agencies across the US federal government have collaborated in the development of the US Climate Resilience Toolkit;[71] this will guide communities in the process by sharing frameworks, databases, and relevant case studies. Previously mentioned examples include community-based organizations like PlaNYC and the San Diego Climate Change Collaborative and emerging networks like 100ResilientCities.

Despite the numerous ways in which you can fortify your home and your community, there are, unfortunately, limits to adaptation. There is not much that can be done to salvage certain coastal properties. Some events will simply penetrate our defenses. Ultimately, we would all be better

---

[70] https://www.usa.gov/elected-officials
[71] http://toolkit.climate.gov/

off if these were issues we didn't have to confront... in other words, if we addressed the causes of man-made climate change rather than trying to adapt to it.

Chapter takeaways:

- There is plenty you can and should do to increase your resilience to climate change.
- Solutions need to be case specific; there is no "one size fits all."
- Be realistic with your choices; pick meaningful, cost-effective measures.
- Understand the limitations of resilience; don't throw good money after bad!
- Be sure to leverage the growing number of resources available to guide you in this process.
- Don't focus solely on your home; be sure to reach out to your elected officials so that community resilience measures are also being deployed.

Chapter 5 – Other Smart Choices

There are two possible future extremes. At this point, we can be certain there would be substantial change in either case. In one future, we fail to address climate change and we struggle adapting to its consequences. In another future—the preferred alternative—we rapidly address climate change by initiating what will inevitably be a profound and radical transformation of entire industries, including energy, transportation, and agriculture.

I suspect the most likely future lies somewhere in between. Whatever the path, change is coming. The previous chapters, focused on the example of property, introduced a sequence of thoughtful questions to help better prepare for the upcoming changes. We can generalize and apply a similar approach to other important decisions, like career choices and financial investments. In both of these examples, by reflecting on climate change, you will not only better manage risks, but simultaneously better position yourself to identify new opportunities.

Imagine you have just finished university. You are about to start your career and have in front of you competing offers. One is to join an oil and gas firm and the other a solar company. Your choice should be guided not only by how you think climate change will evolve, but also by how you think energy policy and demand preferences will evolve as a result.

Scenario A: Imagine that, in the following year, extreme weather batters the country and, in a knee-jerk reaction, Congress enacts policies that crush prospects for oil & gas firms and strongly support investment in clean energy sources.

Scenario B: Imagine that, on the other hand, extreme weather events remain rare for ten or twenty years, and that there are no new initiatives to promote clean energy over fossil fuels. Oil companies continue to be as profitable as ever.

Which is the best job offer? Does your answer change depending on which scenario you think is most likely? Furthermore, would you make this decision from a financial standpoint only, or would you consider other dimensions, such as morality, or how well regarded the two professions are in the eyes of your community and the broader society?

Author's Note: I don't want to mislead you into thinking Scenario B is just as likely as Scenario A; this is just for the purpose of illustration. Personally, I see an escalation of extreme weather over the coming years as being far more likely.

The decisions most people face are not in contexts where climate change is as obvious as the above example. What you need to keep in mind is that the domino effects of climate change are truly far-reaching. Climate change will have severe impacts on many industries, including electric utilities, water utilities, agriculture, fishing, insurance companies, banks, tourism, construction, and all sorts of multinational companies with long interdependent supply chains.

In all cases, you should ask similar questions to those we asked when assessing the desirability of communities and properties. In short, you are better off when companies and their broader industries are devoting resources to assess and prepare for climate change. In instances where this is not the case, your career decisions and investments are at greater risk of being blindsided.

In a previous chapter, I briefly mentioned how fisheries in New England are already suffering from declining fish stocks because of warming oceans. Now consider agriculture. One of California's most profitable crops is the almond, which requires relatively large amounts of water. In 2015, as the state struggled through a multi-year drought, many were questioning the future viability of this crop. It is unlikely everyone who invested in this crop will get a return. Meanwhile, across the Atlantic, Europeans joke that French winemakers may have to migrate to England in pursuit of their beloved climate.

Not long ago, the president of the World Bank warned, "Sooner rather than later, financial regulators must address the systemic risk associated with carbon-intensive activities in their economies. Start now by enforcing disclosure of climate risk and requiring companies and financial institutions to access their exposure to climate-related impacts."[72] At the time of writing, The Bank of England was actually working on a report for the UK government analyzing the risks of a "carbon bubble." Financial regulators are starting to take the issue very seriously. Mark Carney, governor of the Bank of England, has made similar statements. Mr. Carney points out that the risks are not just to equity holders, but to financial institutions as well. Banks may have to write off loans to energy companies if their assets become stranded.[73]

Fortunately, many companies and industries are taking a proactive stance. Iconic brands including Google, Wal-Mart, Nike and Unilever, are going as far as becoming carbon neutral, paving the road for others.[74] Similar efforts can be found in much smaller businesses, including microbrewers and ski resorts. On a grander scale, there are coordinated efforts, such as the Carbon Disclosure Project, which are helping standardize approaches to facilitate the evaluation, comparison, and communication of risks and performance. As part of their standard risk management procedures, companies may opt to act on

---

[72] http://www.worldbank.org/en/news/speech/2014/01/23/world-bank-group-president-jim-yong-kim-remarks-at-davos-press-conference
[73] http://www.bbc.com/news/business-34396969
[74] https://www.whitehouse.gov/the-press-office/2015/10/19/fact-sheet-white-house-announces-commitments-american-business-act

climate change even before their leaders fully comprehend its reality and implications. This would be similar to getting insurance; that is to say, they may choose to do things differently because (a) no matter what they believe is most likely to happen (my house won't burn down), they recognize there is enough of a chance of serious climate change (but it could) to warrant action, and/or (b) regardless, they recognize it is probable that officials will implement new policies and laws to address climate change. The actions of officials can be just as impactful on some companies as climate change disruptions are on others. In the power sector, the costs of meeting EPA regulations designed to reduce emissions is significant, while in the agricultural sector, it is nature itself, in the form of storms, heat and drought, that is most daunting This is not to say that agriculture won't have to cope with new regulations (on water use, for instance), or that power companies won't have to deal with the effects of storms. Most industries, like most communities, will have to face multiple challenges.

You need to be careful, though, when you assess what companies are doing. Public statements don't always equate to action. Some companies may simply be "greenwashing" for public relations. Dig deeper and you'll find they are inadequately prepared. In recent years, all oil and gas majors have publicly defended action on climate change, but then ignored claims of stranded asset risk. In some cases, they have even sold off prior investments in clean energy businesses and financed lobby groups that try to block political action to mitigate climate change.

So far, I have mainly talked of scenarios and probabilities. I wish I could offer you a more narrow range of possible outcomes. I cannot. The best I can do is point the direction. My two cents are that gradually we will see substantial action on climate change as advocacy movements promoting mitigation and adaptation policies continue to gain steam. Though there have been significant lulls, when it seemed like many people forgot about the issue, the trend since the 1990s has been toward taking climate change more seriously and doing more to combat it.

Three factors will continue to fuel the support for action on climate change. First, climate disruptions are becoming more pronounced. As more people experience the effects first hand, existing movements will grow and new ones will emerge. Second, our scientific understanding of the issues is deepening and providing more detail, both in theory/explanation and on-the-ground evidence, which gives everyone increased confidence in projections and warnings. Third, experts both in the field of climate science and the advocacy movement continue to learn, after painful trial and error, how best to communicate our knowledge of climate change, tailoring the message to the distinct communication needs of different audiences.

The above statements describe the general trend. There is also the question of speed, influenced by a myriad of factors. When I started writing this book, for example, oil prices around the world were plummeting, and a new Republican Senate majority, traditionally opposed to action on climate change, was being inaugurated. There are reasons to believe events like these can slow down the adoption of clean energy sources.

The more attuned you are to these developments, the better positioned you are to take advantage of the ensuing opportunities. At this point, climate change is already happening and will, at the very least, continue to a certain degree. We've put a lot of CO2 in the atmosphere and it tends to linger up there. Consequently, there will be growing demand for new services and products!

It is no surprise entrepreneurs have been busy creating a new gamut of companies— from Tesla bringing electric cars back to life to the Climate Corporation developing more sophisticated insurance products for farmers. There are companies developing new business models that make it easy for people and companies to acquire solar. A prominent example is Solar City, which propelled a zero-down solar lease, becoming the largest player in the market. Both utilities and private players have created community solar offerings or "green power" options for people living in apartments who want to ensure their electricity is generated by renewables. You have other companies, such as Stem, pioneering the development of electricity storage. Cost-effective storage would enable renewables to assume a greater share of electricity production. Inevitably, time will tell us more about climate change and how effective we have been in our response, which is a great segue to the following and final chapters.

Other Smart Choices

Chapter takeaways:

- The magnitude of change—whether on account of our inaction or mitigation efforts—is such that it will have profound impacts across the economy.
- Simply attempting to analyze what the impacts might be will help you identify where the opportunities lie.
- Developing and applying this knowledge will help you make smarter career and investment choices.

Chapter 6 – Becoming a Climate Hero

Question: What can I do to stop climate change?
Answer: Plenty!

You can start small and quickly go big. In fact, you can accomplish a great deal with minimal to no changes in your personal lifestyle. Joining this cause is not about turning your back on civilization. It is about helping us transition towards clean technologies... technologies that are emissions-free. This is the very heart of climate change mitigation. Always remember that what you do matters, regardless of who you are. Your actions, even symbolic ones, can influence those of your peers. Your purchasing decisions send signals across entire supply chains, impacting business practices throughout. Your vote and the opinions you share are signals interpreted by politicians trying to decipher which issues to focus on and what stance to take.

Generally speaking, your actions can take place on three levels:
1. At Home
2. In your Community
3. On the National and Global Stages

The types of actions are different, as are their impacts. Some will argue—I, among them—that it is actually on the third level that you can have the most impact with the least amount of effort. Regardless, each of the three is important in its own way.

Level 1: Start small... climate change mitigation at home

You can start by measuring your own carbon footprint and, in the process, learn about the different ways to reduce it. I've grouped examples of the actions available to you into three general areas:

- **Reducing consumption,** with things as basic as turning off the lights, lowering the temperature on your thermostat, washing clothes in cold water instead of warm, and driving less.
- **Switching to low-carbon or carbon-neutral alternatives,** like driving an electric car, installing solar panels and electric batteries, buying "green energy" if it is offered by your utility, avoiding meat as a source of protein, replacing old light bulbs with more efficient technologies like LEDs, and/or replacing old appliances with energy-efficient newer models.
- **Buying carbon offsets** to compensate for your emissions, where your money is used to support projects that reduce emissions elsewhere. Funding might go to reforestation efforts or to the building of installations to burn methane (an extremely potent greenhouse gas) in landfills and on farms. With a quick Google search, you can find many carbon offset providers from which to choose.

In addition, you should keep in mind that every time you make a purchase of any kind, you essentially cast a vote in the market. When a supermarket chain such as Wal-Mart or Target places a sign near a product to single out a specific attribute like "local," "organic," "recycled" or, let's imagine, "carbon free," they very carefully monitor any resulting changes in customer behavior. If the sign contributes to an increase in the relative sales of the demarcated product, then the supermarket may increase the shelf space dedicated to that and similar products. This has ripple effects across the supply chain. Makers of these products and their competitors start changing their operations in order get more of the desired attribute.

In other words, every time you favor a product that makes an effort to be carbon-neutral, you encourage companies to do the same. Several organizations, like the Carbon Trust, are helping consumers and companies do exactly this by developing carbon labels and certification processes. Similar efforts include San Francisco startups like Product Bio, which hopes to leverage big data in order to streamline product lifecycle assessments, helping procurement teams buy from suppliers that adhere to their values and standards. It is unclear at this point which will be the dominant standards or labels recognized by the general public shopping in a typical supermarket. Nonetheless, you should expect to see more carbon labels with the passage of time.

As a personal example, I have opted to buy more clothes from Patagonia. My decision was, to a large extent, a conscious choice to support this iconic brand with its mission to develop zero-impact clothes. Anticipating these trends in consumer behavior and the inherent growth in demand for related information, many companies are trying to disclose their emissions and respective curtailment efforts, as well as the results of these efforts. One of these is Unilever, the parent company of many household brands, including Dove and Ben & Jerry's.

It is important to realize and remember that not all measures are created equal. A couple of long flights overseas can quickly eradicate any gains from replacing your old car with a hybrid. Becoming a vegetarian can have just as much impact as an energy efficiency retrofit of your entire house! It is precisely because most of us lack the experience required to make intuitive decisions about mitigation efforts that I recommend you dedicate 15 minutes to playing around with online carbon footprint calculators. This will help you understand the relative merits of the different options and prioritize accordingly. There are now several free tools available that can provide you a quick assessment with just a few clicks. UC Berkley's Cool Climate Carbon Calculator is one example; the Nature Conservancy's Carbon Footprint Calculator and the EPA's Household Carbon Calculator are others. With another quick Google search, you will be able to find a much larger set of options. Using these tools will also help you find longer lists of ideas to reduce your carbon footprint. You will be doing everyone a favor when you try to reduce your own footprint, even more so when you let others see you. Doing so will put the problem *and the solutions* back on people's radar; making your actions visible makes them real in the minds of others.

Finally, take a step back and reflect on what climate change means for you in the grand scheme of things. At this point, with all that you know, it will likely make its way up to the very top of the list. Keep climate change in mind when you vote in an election. When asked what issues matter to you, answer "climate change" first. If candidates are not serious about climate change, don't vote for them—what kind of leaders would they be anyway?

Level 2: Expand your reach... action on a community scale

While conducting research for my documentary project, *Adaptation Now*, I came across a survey developed by the San Diego Climate Collaborative with an interesting result: "Over 90% (of key influential leaders surveyed) identified themselves as part of a community concerned about climate change in the San Diego region. However, 90% described other San Diego leaders as moderately to not at all concerned."[75] I suspect this is true in most communities, at the office, and perhaps even among members of our own families. This is only possible if people aren't talking about climate change. You can change that. You can put down this book and start a conversation. You can bring it up time and time again to keep it alive. If you need a trigger, get creative and invite your friends over to watch films like *Chasing Ice* or an episode of *Years of Living Dangerously*. These visually stunning documentary projects are bound to get a reaction.

---

[75] https://www.sandiego.edu/climate/documents/KI_2011report.pdf

One evening not too long ago, I was genuinely moved by what I witnessed at a community event in a church in Norfolk, VA. We were filming an educational event put together by an organization called Flood of Voices. Working to spread awareness and mobilize the community of Norfolk to address climate change, they encouraged those attending to come up and share their personal stories of how they were impacted by flooding caused by sea level rise. As you can imagine, at first people were reluctant to walk up to the front of the room. Public speaking is not something everyone enjoys, but after the first person told his story, the mood in the room changed. It transitioned from one of fear of speaking to one of "I too have something to say, I too have something at stake." When people realized they were not alone—that others were just as concerned and just as willing to do something about it—momentum started to build. More volunteers stood up and came forward to tell their stories. With great interest, others started asking questions of the more knowledgeable participants about ongoing efforts in the city and surrounding communities they could join or follow. It was clear we were witnessing the beginning of something remarkable; it was a reminder of the transformational power of people working together for a common purpose.

A lot can be done to advance climate change mitigation at the community level. Many actions that influence how energy is produced, or how transportation systems evolve, or where our food comes from are actually made at the local and regional levels. In 2015, for example, the city council of Portland, Oregon passed a resolution banning future investments in infrastructure to transport or store fossil fuels within the city.[76] Cities can influence or determine how fast utilities in their territory transition to renewable energy. Municipal transportation authorities can

---

[76] http://www.bizjournals.com/portland/blog/sbo/2015/11/portland-passes-resolution-to-oppose-new-fossil.html

invest in zero-emission public-transit systems with the help of companies like Proterra, which makes electric buses and Vision Fleet, which helps finance the investment in electric fleets. It is in your best interest to ensure the right decisions get made. In essence, you need to create political will. You need to let your elected officials and their future contenders know climate change is a priority for you.

There are many ways of accomplishing this; several brave pioneers are already working to advance sensible policies on the frontlines. One group of which I have grown particularly fond is Mothers Out Front. Based on the East Coast of the US, their MO is very much centered on grass-root action brought about by concerned mothers and grandmothers reaching out to their peers. To grow their support base they promote direct outreach to other members of the community. This is sometimes done through the very simple and practical means of hosting house parties. In Massachusetts, Mothers Out Front launched a campaign for the state to meet all of its power needs from renewables, energy efficiency, and conservation. They rallied their members through targeted actions focused on three groups of decision makers: homeowners, community leaders, and state government officials. They pursued concrete goals for each of these groups, such as getting thousands of homeowners to switch to renewable energy and applying pressure on the governor to uphold the targets set in the Massachusetts Global Warming Solutions Act.[77]

Another group that gives me hope, pun intended, is Interfaith Power and Light (IPL). The organization strives to bring together believers of all religions. They are united in their recognition that their beliefs require them to be "faithful stewards of creation."[78] In that light, they work to address global warming through their congregations. Actions go beyond educational initiatives; they also involve

---

[77] http://www.mothersoutfront.org/
[78] http://www.interfaithpowerandlight.org/

reducing the carbon footprint of those same congregations and making them role models for the adoption of energy efficiency and renewable energy solutions. On a policy front, the organization first develops positions on numerous related issues. It then mobilizes its members through actions like targeted petitions, such as requests to Pope Francis to order the Vatican Bank to divest from all investments in fossil fuels.

Not everyone is comfortable talking about climate change directly or participating in community events. If that describes you, there is still plenty you can do. In fact, you can be just, if not more, effective exerting a positive influence in your community indirectly. You can write op-eds for your local paper and letters to your elected officials. You can practice first with online posts in an environment that is more contained and familiar to you. A well-written letter, article, or blog post can go a long way. As mentioned earlier, the US government makes it easy for you to reach out to your officials by listing their contacts online. Just visit the government website page on How to Contact Elected Officials and you'll get access to everyone from the offices of local county officials to the White House.[79] Similarly, almost all major publications have instructions online for how to submit letters to the editor.

One group that does this particularly well is Citizen's Climate Lobby (CCL). After quick orientation calls and connecting people through a growing network of local chapters, CCL provides volunteers with the resources to become effective advocates. These resources include contacts, a caring support network, "laser" talking points, and evidence to back up these points. In addition, they help their members tailor their messages to a wide set of relevant stakeholders. Over time, CCL has built an impressive database of the issues that matter most for communities and politicians across the US. They are incredibly effective, accomplishing a great deal with small

---

[79] https://www.usa.gov/elected-officials

means. Such is their success that people in other countries have proactively volunteered to set up local chapters, fueled by nothing but sheer determination. These volunteers hope to apply the same underlying strategies and tactics as those embraced by CCL in the US, adjusting them to the local political constructs. It seems like every year the organization doubles in size, as does its reach, measured in terms of meetings with Congressional offices and letters written to elected officials and/or published by mainstream media.[80]

There is an enormous advantage to working with others. It goes beyond sharing knowledge about what is working and what is not. At the very least, you will keep each other motivated when the going gets rough... and it will! Ask veterans of the climate change movement if they ever get tired or frustrated, and you will often hear how they thought the problem would have been resolved decades ago! Let me reiterate this point: I strongly recommend that you join existing movements. There is no point in reinventing the wheel or spinning your wheels. Finally, the more coordinated and synchronized calls for action are, the more effective they will be. By working together you will find you have a much louder voice. Groups like Citizens Climate Lobby will help you learn how best to talk about climate change, especially when you are addressing someone who doesn't feel comfortable talking about it. As one of my favorite professors used to say, quoting his father, "Learn from other people's mistakes; you won't live long enough to learn them all yourself."

The Yale Climate Change Communication Project has done a great job of studying how people's understanding of climate change can differ, and what that means in terms of how you should talk to them when approaching the subject. One of their landmark studies was the *6 Americas Report*, in which they split the population of the United States into six segments along a spectrum of belief and

---

[80] https://citizensclimatelobby.org/

motivation. In 2012, when the first report came out, they had, on one end, the "Alarmed," which consisted of 16 percent of the population and were the people most likely to act on climate change. On the other end were the "Dismissive," which consisted of 12 percent of the population and were, for lack of a better word, the deniers. The majority of people were somewhere in between.

One of the benefits of this kind of segmentation is that it enables people to tailor their message in a way that makes it more effective. It wouldn't make much sense to spend your time discussing the science of climate change to someone who is already "Alarmed." When talking to people who are already motivated to act on climate change, you should emphasize solutions they can undertake or support. In contrast, if you are talking to a true denier, your best option is to stop talking and conserve your energy for the people who will reason with you.

When talking to people in the middle of the spectrum, you probably need to do more groundwork before jumping to solutions and recommendations for action. They won't fully understand climate change, its causes, or its consequences. They won't be as informed as you at this point. Once again, by being part of an existing group, you can leverage the group's experience and resulting know-how. It will help you more quickly become an effective communicator who knows how to tailor his/her approach to the situation. You are more likely to have access to relevant and impactful stories. You are more likely to learn talking points that recognize basic tenets of behavioral science, such as the facts that the most people are more responsive to stories than data, and that each of us has a tendency to conform to social norms. You are more likely to receive helpful guidance, such as the recommendation to focus your efforts on people with whom you can connect and bond over shared values and experience.

Becoming a Climate Hero

Your efforts don't necessarily have to be focused on your neighbors or fellow members of your congregation. You can have tremendous impact within your profession. One example alluded to earlier involved the American Society of Civil Engineers, which created a committee on climate change. Perhaps their actions will result in more rapid reform of building codes across the nation. Another example is the CDC investing in training for health professionals, in order to be better prepared for the effects of climate change on human health.[81]

Community level actions can and should take place at work, or be oriented towards the businesses that serve you. Business leaders and their decisions can have huge impacts on emissions, both directly and indirectly. Just like homeowners, businesses can influence how much energy they consume and where that energy is coming from. Businesses also tend to have influence over government policies and politicians. Always remember: business leaders are just as susceptible as elected officials to pressure from the public and their employees. The more you ask of them on this front, the greater their incentive to change. Conversely, the less you ask of them, the more likely we are to continue with business as usual.

A great deal of work has been done to study the benefits to organizations of becoming serious about climate change and, in a broader sense, sustainability. When I write "becoming serious," I am referring to the adoption of truly meaningful measures that go beyond a few symbolic gestures used for public relations purposes, often critically known as "greenwashing." You can leverage and refer to these benefits to build a compelling argument that will persuade and inspire your work peers to join the cause.

There is a business case for action based on gains to operational efficiencies alone. Internal climate change mitigation measures can lower costs for businesses and

---

[81] http://www.cdc.gov/nceh/information/climate_and_health.htm

increase profits. A common example is investing in energy efficiency to reduce electricity consumption at factories and offices. Changes to things like lighting, heating and cooling systems, and/or building insulation can offer businesses attractive returns on investment. Other business-controlled levers include policies that impact travel and people's daily commutes. Furthermore, in the United States and elsewhere, more and more businesses are finding it profitable to invest in onsite solar generation and storage systems.

Operational efficiencies are only the beginning. The implementation of a sustainability agenda with specific initiatives and strong communication has positives impacts on key success factors such as employee retention and overall engagement. It contributes to the creation of a purpose-driven culture of which employees can be proud, translating into a more productive work environment.

Finally, there is a strategic rationale that prompts businesses to go beyond measures with an immediate or relatively certain payoff. Harvard Business School professor Rebecca Henderson writes in her working paper *Making the Business Case for Environmental Sustainability*, "for many firms, the case for sustainable change is better understood as a strategic bet against a number of possible future states." Professor Henderson explains in her paper, through illustrative future scenarios and present day examples, how possible changes to consumer preferences, technology, and regulatory or political constructs can make sustainability a calculated strategic priority for business leaders.

Don't wait for leadership to act if they haven't already. Don't settle for mediocre "greenwashing" if that is all that is being done. Businesses are often focused on the priorities of their largest customers and anchored by organizational habits. They can miss out on opportunities, even those in plain sight. For climate change to rise to the top of the strategic agenda, there needs to be a voice from within… it can start with you. Think about using the appropriate forums to express ideas. Join or start a group with your peers to discuss the opportunities for the company and how to implement them. Be brave and ask for support from the company's leadership. Many of the most successful initiatives at the companies I've worked with have strong employee roots. More often than not, leadership teams are thrilled to have employees take charge of value-creating ideas.

As you embark on this journey to promote climate action in your communities, you will no doubt benefit from additional resources to help answer questions that will be asked along the way. You will be happy to know there is no shortage of publicly available resources, case studies, and role models. Their depth and breadth continues to grow, as does the quality of the content they produce and events they organize. I have listed several resources in the bibliography of this book, but for now, here are a few of my personal favorites:

- Skeptical Science ranks the most common arguments by people questioning the reality of climate change, such as "it's the sun," or "the climate has changed before," and provides you with a summarized and evidence-based response.[82]
- The Guardian, a daily newspaper based in the United Kingdom (with an online US edition), does a great job of covering global news on all facets of climate change.[83]
- There is also the ClearPath Foundation, based in Charlotte, NC, and launched by entrepreneur Jay Faison in 2015, with a moderate-to-conservative audience in mind. Noticing that climate change was too intertwined and confused with other objectives of "crazy environmentalists," Jay's team is approaching the issues with an alternative

---

[82] #http://www.skepticalscience.com/
[83] http://www.theguardian.com/environment/climate-change

conservative mindset. As he writes, "What could be more conservative than energy independence and freeing up energy markets that were controlled by monopolies?"[84]

Level 3: Go big! Action on the National and Global Stages

Actions on an individual level will largely be educational; they'll also give you green credentials and confidence. Actions on the community level will help you become an effective advocate, but it won't be enough to move the needle. Applying your efforts to the national and global stages is how you can have the most impact. This doesn't require a big shift or extra work; the tools of the trade are the same as on level 2. What it does require is focus and coordination in terms of what you advocate for, whom you advocate to, and whom you advocate with. At this level, it is a numbers game.

As explained at the beginning of this book, it really doesn't matter where emissions come from. This means all communities across the globe must become emissions-free. This is a system-wide challenge and, as such, it requires system-based solutions. Alone, our actions are just not enough. While this makes the challenge before us difficult, difficult is not impossible. At the end of the day it simply must be done. The cost of the alternative—the cost of inaction—is unacceptable. We are all in this together.

It grows dimmer every day, but there is light at the end of the tunnel, urging us to move fast. More than anything else, we need a price on carbon. This is the silver bullet. You can play an active and critical role in making it happen. You can do so with minimal effort. That is how you can make a real difference. A price on carbon is a marvelous thing. It triggers the innovation and relentless efficiency of market forces in the pursuit of the best

---

[84] http://www.clearpath.org/

solutions to eradicate carbon from our way of life. It does so in a way that is consistent with the idiosyncrasies of different countries, regions, industries, and companies.

I can't tell you that electric cars are better than hydrogen fuel-celled cars, or that the solution to our transportation needs is biofuels. Perhaps, in the end, the winning technology will be some form of carbon capture and sequestration that allows us to continue using fossil fuels. I find that unlikely, but I recognize the possibility.

What I can tell you is that a price on carbon is what can best determine the optimal mix. I am certainly not alone in thinking this way; surveys of economists find there is wide support for this measure. The World Bank and IMF actively promote it as a governing priority, convening powerful political leaders (like German Chancellor Angela Merkel) through purposefully created organizations (like the Carbon Pricing Panel) to call on their peers to support carbon-pricing initiatives.[85] Institutional investors—such as BlackRock and CalPERS, representing trillions of dollars of investments (more than the GDP of the United States)—have also joined the call for a price on carbon through CERES, an organization mobilizing business leaders for a sustainable world.[86] Even major oil and gas firms publicly support it, as voiced by Ben van Beurden, the CEO of Shell.[87]

In a working paper entitled *Corporate Leaders Need to Step Up on Climate Change*, Harvard Business School professor Michael Toffel and Aspen Snowmass VP of Sustainability Auden Schendler argued that the only serious corporate sustainability program is one that has climate change as its priority and includes advocacy for

---

[85] http://www.worldbank.org/en/programs/pricing-carbon

[86] http://www.ceres.org/press/press-releases/world2019s-leading-institutional-investors-managing-24-trillion-call-for-carbon-pricing-ambitious-global-climate-deal

[87] http://www.forbes.com/sites/sciencebiz/2014/09/23/why-this-big-oil-ceo-believes-in-applying-a-price-to-carbon/

political solutions such as "carbon fee and dividends." In its absence, a corporate sustainability program is not really meaningful. I think this summarizes my own position extremely well.

Ultimately, only governments can implement a system-wide price on carbon. While it is conceptually easy, it can get complicated very quickly. It is not the purpose of this book to suggest how a price on carbon should be implemented; that is a political process. The purpose of this book is to encourage you to ask your elected officials to jumpstart the process.

Note, climate change has been given much attention and there is no shortage of proposed solutions out there. Many of them, seeking to minimize the bureaucracy and maximize the effectiveness of a carbon price, are already being tested and refined. According to the World Bank, there were— in 2015—over 40 countries and 20 cities, states, and/or provinces that had implemented, or were planning to implement, a price on carbon. The largest of these includes the European Emissions Trading Scheme, which spans the EU and a few neighboring countries like Norway. There is also a regional cap and trade model in the United States, which includes ten Northeastern and Mid-Atlantic states.[88] A key milestone was the announcement, made by China's President Xi Jinping in the run-up to the December 2015 Paris Climate Talks, that China plans on implementing a nationwide cap and trade program by 2017.[89]

In 2008, the Canadian province of British Columbia launched North America's first carbon tax. They made it "revenue neutral" by requiring that the proceeds raised be returned to the public through income and corporate tax breaks. The rate of about $30 (Canadian) per carbon

---

[88] http://www.worldbank.org/en/programs/pricing-carbon
[89] http://www.forbes.com/sites/mclifford/2015/09/30/chinas-xi-jinping-announces-cap-and-trade-carbon-program-will-it-work/

tonne is applied to fossil fuels used in transportation, electricity generation, and heating. The tax proved to meaningfully reduce the consumption of fuel in the province—16 percent by 2014—while the local economy continued to grow.[90]

Along these lines is an exemplary solution being promoted by Citizens Climate Lobby, a non-partisan organization advocating for the implementation of a federal carbon fee and dividend. They propose a steadily rising fee imposed at the point of extraction (the oil well) and encompassing border adjustments (in case foreign nations don't have their own fees). The revenue from the fee would then be distributed back to households, so as not to grow government, using existing infrastructure like social security.[91] They have methodically and thoughtfully developed a proposal that is compatible with the political preferences on both sides of the aisle. It is impossible not to like these guys; they remind me of how democracy is supposed to work and of how committed citizens can help balance the scale against vested interests. They simply know how to do.

So... Go big! Add your voice to those of other climate heroes. Politicians prioritize public opinion. What we need to do is make sure climate change is at the very top of the list. This will require immense discipline and focus. We need to state our requests and repeat them until they are heard. As Mark Reynolds, the Executive Director of Citizens Climate Lobby, stated, "When you are trying to do the impossible, you need laser-like focus."

---

[90] http://www.economist.com/blogs/americasview/2014/07/british-columbias-carbon-tax
[91] https://citizensclimatelobby.org/carbon-fee-and-dividend/

Chapter takeaways:

- Start small. Go online to estimate your carbon footprint and learn about how to reduce it.
- Take it up a level. Join an existing organization working on climate change mitigation projects (like Citizens Climate Lobby). On the odd chance you can't find one that works for you, create your own and build a supportive community.
- Go big! Learn how to reach your elected officials and effectively advocate for a price on carbon. Start by writing a letter; the writing process alone will act as a powerful forcing mechanism for organizing your thoughts.

Chapter 7 - Mitigation Roadmap - Achieving Focus

By implementing the actions outlined in Chapter 6, you will have profound impact. But what if you want to do more, because you realize there is a lot to do? What if you want to double down and are eager to know how you can have the biggest impact possible? In essence, you want to be sure that you are applying your energy wisely, focusing it on the measures that have the highest chances of success, the measures that will ultimately move the needle.

In the case of climate change, the needle is the global rate of anthropogenic (manmade) GHG emissions, measured in parts per million. The question of focus is a critical one at our current juncture. There are now countless organizations throughout the world working on climate change, but our collective efforts have yet to be effective. As observed in Chapter 1, emissions are still on the rise, even though we've known about the risks of climate change for decades. The safety threshold for the atmospheric concentration of CO2 was 350 parts per million. In 2015, we surpassed 400 parts per million, and were set to surpass 1°C of warming. Reversing this trend is our goal.

First, **each one of us should be thoughtful and honest in order to identify distractions and avoid spinning our wheels.**

As many executive coaches will tell you, being busy does not equate to being productive. It may seem like I'm contradicting myself, but I want you to know that I am not a fan of small measures, particularly when these measures are implemented by themselves. Changing the light bulbs helps, but if you think you are finished... that you have contributed your fair share... then you are mistaken. If all of us only do a little, then we will collectively only achieve a little.

By examining some of the ongoing efforts to address climate change, we can identify how some of them have the potential for becoming distractions. I find two examples particularly dangerous because they appear to promise salvation. I want to be fair and say upfront that these two case studies are positive efforts with the very best of intentions; they make meaningful contributions to mitigate climate change. In that regard, they have my full support. Unfortunately, from my perspective, they are also fundamentally flawed; they have structural limitations that constrain their full potential.

Case Study #1: There is a lot of emphasis on improving energy efficiency. Energy efficiency reduces emissions and usually saves people money in the process. In many instances, implementing energy efficiency measures is a no-brainer. In 2007, McKinsey & Co, a major global strategy consulting firm, published its first—and now world-renowned—greenhouse gas abatement curve. The curve measures cost effectiveness by demonstrating the abatement potential of each initiative, including their CO_2 emissions reduction potential and cost. The "cost" might actually be negative, if the initiative actual generates money or savings, which is the case with many energy efficiency measures like replacing old light bulbs with LEDs.[92]

While energy efficiency measures are the low-hanging fruit of climate change mitigation measures, they are, unfortunately, severely limited, because we will always need more energy. While we continue to find ways of doing what we did before with less energy, we will still end up doing more things overall. It's human nature. As living standards improve, new technologies are discovered, and economies grow around the world—as they should—we will consume more energy than we do now. Projections by

---

[92]http://www.mckinsey.com/client_service/sustainability/latest_thinking/greenhous e_gas_abatement_cost_curves

expert bodies like International Energy Agency (IEA) continue to show increases in energy consumption.[93]

I stated "as they should," and I want to make this point with a less abstract and more concrete example. I am a huge fan of international travel, which has a relatively big carbon footprint. I believe, nonetheless, that travel yields incalculable benefits that are hard to achieve with alternatives. When millions of Chinese tourists visit Japan, that interaction helps bridge old and dangerous divides. It literally brings people together, which can establish the bonds of peace. The world is better off when more people travel and when they get to travel more, so we need to find climate change solutions that allow for more travel. It is encouraging that some airlines are trying to do exactly that. Richard Branson is the founder of the Virgin Group, which includes Virgin America and Virgin Atlantic. He is also a strong advocate for action on climate change. Branson went as far as committing all of the group's profits from travel for a ten-year period to investments in groundbreaking technologies, with the potential to make the aviation industry "one of the cleanest."

The takeaway from this case study is that our best minds and resources should be directed at measures that allow us to make energy without emitting carbon and other greenhouse gases. We should not be prioritizing options that, by design, cannot solve the underlying problem. I am fundamentally in favor of energy efficiency and don't want to discourage it. It is a step in the right direction. What I don't want is for energy efficiency to be the flagship of mitigation efforts. Ultimately, we need to collectively prioritize the solutions that can get the job done.

Case Study #2 Since the Earth Summit in Rio back in 1992, world leaders and their delegates have been negotiating goals, metrics, targets, strategies, and mechanisms that underpin global "treaties" to address

---

[93] http://www.worldenergyoutlook.org/

climate change. These sessions have historically culminated in what are called COP meetings, or Conference of the Parties. Important decisions and commitments are made through this forum, such as trying to limit the increase in average global temperature to 2°C.

Trying to achieve a consensus that is both binding and meaningful has been an arduous and frustrating task, in part because it requires too many parties facing very distinct economic and socio-political realities to agree. Additionally, it is incredibly difficult to hold nation-states to their commitment. The Kyoto Protocol in 1997 was an attempt to get countries to commit to legally binding targets. As a result, some countries opted not to ratify it like the United States, and others withdrew from it later on like Canada.

One of the points of disagreement at these conferences involved who should pay for emerging markets to adopt clean energy technologies, which have historically been more costly than conventional fossil fuel-based alternatives. The underlying argument presented by emerging markets was that climate change was not their fault. Consequently, when it comes to addressing climate change, they thought it unfair to "pay" a share equal to that of developed nations. They were referring not only to higher energy costs (ignoring the social costs of fossil fuels), but also to the potential for subsequent losses in GDP.

To be more precise, climate change is not just a question of flow, but also one of stock. This is because once CO_2 is in the atmosphere, it lingers there for a long time, from decades to centuries. At the beginning of the industrial revolution, the concentration of CO_2 was around 280 parts per million. Most of the emissions that got us to 400 parts per million are attributed to Europe and the United States. It was the growth of these economies, powered by fossil fuels, that tapped out the atmosphere's ability to absorb CO2.

In December of 2015, Paris hosted the 21st COP meeting. At COP21 in Paris, and during the preceding months, governments submitted voluntary pledges to cut emissions; these Nationally Determined Contributions (INDCs) are "rooted in domestic priorities and realities."[94] It was hoped that this approach would be more successful than a stringent top-down treaty. The United States, for example, pledged to reduce greenhouse gas emissions 26 percent from 2005 levels by 2025. Concurrently, China pledged that its emissions would peak by 2030. From the perspective of getting an agreement and creating momentum, the approach was effective. Collectively, the Paris pledges surpassed all previous agreements to reduce global emissions. Unfortunately, they also fell short. The cumulative result of the INDCs is not enough to keep global average temperature from increasing beyond 2°C. In addition, because they are voluntary pledges, there is concern countries do not have enough incentives to meet their targets.

There were, however, several immensely positive outcomes from the 2015 Paris Agreement signed by nearly 200 countries at the COP21.[95] Among them was the decision to review each country's pledges every five years; the intent is to keep the momentum going and have peer-pressure be the force that prevents countries from not only reneging on previous pledges, but also from coming up short and not presenting more ambitious targets each time they meet. Linked to this, countries also agreed to set common standards for reporting and tracking progress. Together, these measures send a powerful signal to all participants in the global economy—including investors in the energy sector: carbon pollution must go.

---

[94] http://unfccc.int/focus/indc_portal/items/8766.php
[95] http://www.cop21.gouv.fr/en/195-countries-adopt-the-first-universal-climate-agreement/

In Chapter 6 we discussed how the silver bullet for climate change mitigation is an effective price on carbon. This is the most desirable outcome from such meetings, but an unlikely one. In September 2014, I attended a private webinar with Christiana Figueres, the head of the United Nations Framework Convention on Climate Change. I asked her if she agreed that implementing a carbon price would be the single most powerful measure to mitigate climate change. Her answer was "Yes." She added, however, that the current political environment wouldn't allow it. In light of this political reality, Figueres stated that her hope was for carbon price initiatives to continue to emerge on a regional level. Figueres suggested a more plausible outcome was that they would gradually emerge over time. In other words, she saw the final solution more likely emerging from the bottom-up instead of coming from the top-down.

The general takeaway from this second case study is that if you pin all your hopes on getting everyone to agree, you risk it becoming too late. Since these negotiations started back in Rio, emissions have actually gone up. According to *The Economist,* "Between 2000 and 2010 the rise in greenhouse-gas emissions was even faster than in the 1980s and 1990s."[96] In this way, these global negotiations can also be classified as a potential distraction, despite all the pomp and circumstance. They do, however, grant us small incremental victories that buy us time and build momentum. They also put the media's spotlight on the issue of climate change, which helps create awareness. Finally, they provide a massive forum for the exchange of ideas and a platform for new partnerships. In fact, a lot of promising commitments and measures proposed at COP21 took place on the sidelines of the main deal and came from the private sector and subnational entities like cities and states. These are all immensely powerful levers. All of us working on climate change, myself included,

---

[96] http://www.economist.com/sites/default/files/20151128_climate_change.pdf

continue to hope these global meetings will ultimately be successful, but it is far too risky to just sit and wait for that to happen.

In fact, because the International Agreement signed in Paris was not legally binding— there are no penalties for countries failing to meet their targets —I would argue it is up to the citizens of each country to make them binding by applying pressure as voters. Citizens need to demand during elections that their leaders and successors adhere to their country's commitments and make the necessary additional commitments to make our society carbon neutral in good time. They need to penalize those politicians who fail to deliver by voting them out of office. Politicians are more likely to respond to internal pressure from their voters than they are to international pressure from other countries. Furthermore, many of these politicians would welcome the support from voters on climate action because they depend on the broad support of public movements as much or more than the movements depend on them. Politicians are not white knights...they require consensus in order to successfully implement the measures that reduce greenhouse gas emissions. They know they will face immense pushback from vested interests in the energy sector. They are also aware that many relevant decisions are outside of their authority because they fall under the jurisdiction of local leaders.

Combined, these two case studies teach us a valuable lesson, namely, the importance of thinking about solutions to climate change in terms of their opportunity costs. Opportunity cost is an important concept in economics, useful for making decisions. It means the loss of potential gains from alternatives to the choices we make. To illustrate, before you decide to spend the afternoon reading—knowing how much you will enjoy it— first think about the activities you are giving up, and make sure they wouldn't be more enjoyable. What you are giving up is the opportunity cost of reading. In the case of climate change, each of us needs to be more diligent in thinking about our own options in terms of their opportunity costs.

Second, we should adopt frameworks purposefully designed to help us achieve greater focus when making decisions and allocating our collective resources.

It's time to define a simple strategy and roadmap. A good framework can enable the necessary focus for us to "do the *nearly* impossible" but essential. It does so by narrowing our options, establishing a sequence for our intended actions, and clarifying how we measure success at each step along the way. In this manner, we will know whether we are on track toward achieving our goal. If not, we know we need to quickly adjust.

I recently participated in an offsite strategy session for a solar company. The other executives and I hired a management guru to help us increase our focus and align people across the company. We may have been operating on a completely different scale, but the challenges were similar to those of the climate change movement, particularly the challenge of making meaningful progress towards incredibly ambitious goals. Company employees—including those in management—were growing increasingly frustrated. The common theme was feeling scattered and, consequently, unproductive. The framework with which we worked was the Strategy Map, developed by HBS professor Robert Kaplan.[97] The rules and process for developing the map helped the group develop a comprehensive and succinct punch list that we could enthusiastically execute. All participants left the offsite feeling reinvigorated. We had clarity. We had a shared understanding of what was needed. We had a shared understanding of our individual roles. We were once again ready to roll up our sleeves.

---

[97] https://hbr.org/2000/09/having-trouble-with-your-strategy-then-map-it

Mitigation Roadmap – Achieving Focus

In layman's terms, the map is developed essentially working backwards. You first define your destination, and then define the necessary steps to get there by walking backwards to your starting position. The structure of this map was defined for business applications, but, with a few modifications, we can develop a comparable and tailored solution to the climate movement. At the top of the map is the ultimate measure of success. For a company, this is typically a set of financial indicators around profitability. In our case, it is annual global greenhouse gas emissions. Our goal is simple: zero emissions by 2050.

If we take this goal to be our destination and then take one step back, we can identify what needs to happen before this is possible. By 2050, all our energy and food production needs must be met by emission-free technologies. This means that in the run-up to 2050, we need to aggressively accelerate the replacement of fossil fuel infrastructure with emission-free energy sources, such as solar power, wind power and— potentially—nuclear power. In the cases where we opt to maintain fossil fuel infrastructure (if any), we will needed to install carbon capture and sequestration solutions.

How is this possible? Take another step back and we are at the point where we must create the conditions necessary for this rapid and large-scale adoption of clean energy solutions. When decision makers are given the option between renewable energy and fossil fuels, the prevailing conditions must make it so they always pick renewable energy. The mechanism to make this happen is the implementation of regional carbon prices. We need politicians at the regional and national level to finally address the biggest market failure of all time. The magnitude and nature of this challenge demands a response from our elected leaders. Don't let them off the hook; this is their job!

Measures complementary to the implementation of a price on carbon should also be taken. Additional ways of creating favorable conditions for the transition to a clean energy economy include government support for research and development efforts and the promotion of entrepreneurship focused on clean energy solutions. There are many ways in which governments can provide a boost to these efforts, from direct funding and tax breaks to indirect measures, such as making changes to educational curriculums and/or removing "red tape" from the path of these entrepreneurs. In the run-up to COP21, Bill Gates was an active critic of the low levels of funding going into energy research (relative to other sectors of the economy). Together with other private investors, he committed over $1 billion to start a new clean energy-focused investment fund.[98]

Among the measures that governments should consider putting in place are programs to help workers in fossil fuel industries—and communities dependent on fossil fuels—in their transition to a clean energy economy. These communities are at risk of a double whammy; there will be the impacts of climate change and there will be hardship if new businesses don't grow fast enough to replace those in decline.

By doing these things, we can make clean energy solutions the obvious choice. In many cases, it is already happening. Not too long ago, solar power was prohibitively expensive. Solar power is now a force to be reckoned with in the United States. Cases of grid parity (when solar power becomes competitive with or more economical than existing power sources) are on the rise in the United States and around the world. This has been possible because the price of solar equipment has fallen dramatically with economies of scale, learning curves, and better technology. In addition, business model innovation

---

[98] http://www.breakthroughenergycoalition.com/en/index.html

enabled lowering the other costs of installing solar, including selling, financing, and distribution.

I am extremely passionate about the potential for distributed solar power and devote a great deal of my time working to advance it. I see it as having the ability to democratize electricity generation by giving individuals, businesses, and communities more control over something that has heretofore been determined centrally by governments, regulators, and giant utilities. If its potential is large in the United States, it is even greater in emerging economies, where it can leapfrog conventional grids and power plants (much like mobile phones did with landlines in places like India and Africa where many people's first and only phone is a mobile). We are only now starting to explore the potential of decentralized energy resources that couple solar with battery storage and microgrids.

Overall, when it comes to making clean energy viable, much is owed to the sense of purpose and the perseverance of thousands of entrepreneurs and dedicated professionals working within their realms of expertise. Companies like Tesla and entrepreneurs like Elon Musk have helped prove an alternative reality exists and is within our reach. The Tesla Model S was named the car of the year for two years in a row… not the best electric car, but the best car![99] It is now easy to see a world where the entire fleet of automobiles is electric, because it has been proven that electric cars can perform better than those with combustion engines.

As a result, there are now several efforts to develop more comprehensive regional roadmaps for transitioning to a complete clean energy model. One example is the Solutions Project, which, using research from Stanford University and the work of professor Mark Jacobson (one of its board members), has attempted to design a complete 100 percent renewable energy model for all 50 US states.[100]

---

[99] http://time.com/3721049/tesla-model-s-consumer-reports-car/

Now, take a third and final step back. You are one step away from the starting point, the point at which this book was first written. This is the first step and it is all about creating the political will for urgent and immediate action. Ultimately, this is about mobilizing the voters who form the political base. Politicians will act once it is clear climate change is a priority for voters. This first step is, in essence, about creating awareness and building grassroots support. It is about getting people to understand what is at stake. It is about helping them develop an informed opinion and preparing them to take action, primarily by voting with climate change as the deciding factor when choosing among candidates. This is why Chapter 6, "Becoming a Climate Hero," is the most important chapter in this book. The key to jumpstarting our mission, and sustaining it through to its success, is getting as many people as possible to start the journey of becoming a climate hero.

Once a simple strategy map is defined, like the one proposed above, it is then enhanced with metrics to gauge the level of progress at each step of the way. The ideal number is one or two for each step on the map. With more metrics, you start to lose the focus you've attained. Consider the following proposal, in the order of the steps outlined above:

> Step 1: Recruiting Climate Heroes—Increase the percentage of people who, during an election, prioritize addressing climate change and implementing a carbon price.
> Step 2: Creating Favorable Conditions for Clean Energy—Increase the percentage of the world economy that operates with an "effective" carbon price. By "effective," I mean a price that is meaningful enough to both influence choices and to be applicable to all sources of emissions.

---

[100] http://thesolutionsproject.org/

Step 3: Deploying Clean Energy Solutions—Increase the percentage of installed generation capacity that is emissions free and the percentage of our transportation fleet that is emissions free.

Step 4: Stopping Climate Change—Decrease the amount of global annual GHG emissions, ultimately to zero.

For each of these metrics, we also need to define target success levels and interim goals that enable us to measure our rate of progress. In Step 4, it is zero emissions by 2050, but we can expand on this point by aiming for peak emissions around, let's say, 2025. Naturally, we can expand on this set of metrics and add complementary ones, and then break them down by geography (countries) or industry (electric power, agriculture, transportation...) and so forth. This baseline was like the map itself, deliberately simplified for the purposes of illustration and because of the need for more focus in the climate movement. The important thing is to be directionally correct, not anchoring our actions around false precision.

Third, with the strategy map as our reference, each of us needs to decide how to make the biggest difference.

The map helps us identify what really needs to get done. Using the map, we can prioritize our options, feel confident about dedicating our time to solving climate change, and become a true climate hero. If your strength is people, then help create and spread awareness. If you love technology and building businesses, then join the Elon Musks of this world, people who are trying to develop and commercialize the next generation of climate-friendly solutions. If you are a gifted writer, public speaker, and/or natural leader, then you might consider political action. If you need help establishing momentum and making this a habit, then start your own climate journal, where—every Monday night, for example—you write down what you've done for climate change the week before. It can be something simple, like reading an article or starting a conversation with a friend.

Your choice of paths may not be obvious, and it will probably involve some trial and error. I know this from experience. Solving climate change is, at this point, one of the great pursuits of my life. I have course-corrected after realizing I wasn't making meaningful progress; in fact, that is why I left a career in management consulting. It is likely I will have to pivot again in the future. Even today, I approach the problem from multiple angles; there is the documentary... and this book... and my work in the solar industry. Which of these efforts will prove the most meaningful? I do not know, but I like to think I will keep trying until the job is done.

Chapter takeaways:

- Be precise with how you allocate your time. Remember, it is far more important to convince elected officials of the importance of climate change than it is to replace your light bulbs at home.
- The cornerstone of an effective strategy is the implementation of carbon prices at the regional and national levels.
- Based on your relative strengths and available resources, determine how to contribute. Remember to stage your efforts (order matters).
- If it is unclear how best to proceed, don't be afraid to try different things.
- Start a climate journal.

--

I hope this book has helped you realize the dangers we collectively face by continuing to ignore the changes in our climate. I hope this knowledge empowers you to make smarter decisions, ones that increase your resilience in a potentially harsh future. I hope you become an active participant in a discussion that, whether you knew it or not, involves you. Finally, I hope you are inspired to take the first step on the path to becoming a climate hero.

Before you put this book to rest, I am going to ask you for one small, but surprisingly effective, favor. Please spend the next five minutes answering a simple question: What three things do you plan on doing to address climate change?

Bibliography

I want to express my greatest appreciation to the following people for sharing their experience and observations. Most of the interviews and conversations were conducted while researching for the documentary project *Adaptation Now* prior to commencing the book.

Ada Christensen
Ashley Perl
Auden Schendler
Bill Ritter
Christine Luong
Dan Abbasi
Danny Richter
Elli Sparks
Jeff Lukas
Joe Bouchard
Joyce Coffee
Kate Gordon
Katharine Mach
Kelsey Wirth
Mark Jacobson
Mark Reynolds
Marshall Saunders
Mike Toffel
Rebecca Henderson
Rich Powell
Roger Pulwarty
Skip Stiles
Teresa Stanley
Veva Deheza

Works Cited:

Ahmed, Kamal. "Bank of England Governor - Global Economy at Risk from Climate Change." *BBC News*, 29 Sept. 2015. Web. 14 Nov. 2015.
<http://www.bbc.com/news/business-34396969>.

Bibliography

"Arctic Change: Global - Global Temperature Trends: 2014 Summation." *A Near-Realtime Arctic Change Indicator Website*. The National Oceanic and Atmospheric Administration, n.d. Web. 30 Oct. 2015. <http://www.arctic.noaa.gov/detect/global-temps.shtml>

Barnejee, Neela, Lisa Song, and David Hasemyer. "Exxon: The Road Not Taken." *Inside Climate News*, 16 Sept. 2015. Web. 20 Sept. 2015. <http://insideclimatenews.org/content/Exxon-The-Road-Not-Taken>.

Benton, Tim, and Rob Bailey. "Extreme Weather and Food Shocks." *The New York Times*, 08 Sept. 2015. Web. 14 Nov. 2015. <http://www.nytimes.com/2015/09/09/opinion/extreme-weather-and-food-shocks.html?_r=1>.

Betts, Alexander, et al. *The State of the World's Refugees 2006: Human Displacement in the New Millennium.* Oxford: Oxford UP, 2006. UNHCR's Division of External Relations, n.d. Web 5 Sept. 2015. <http://www.unhcr.org/4a4dc1a89.html>.

Briggs, Helen. "Global CO2 Emissions 'stalled' in 2014." *BBC News*, 13 Mar. 2015. Web. 30 Oct. 2015. <http://www.bbc.com/news/science-environment-31872460>.

Bump, Philip. "Jim Inhofe's Snowball Has Disproven Climate Change Once and for All." *The Washington Post*, 26 Feb. 2015. Web. 14 Nov. 2015. <https://www.washingtonpost.com/news/the-fix/wp/2015/02/26/jim-inhofes-snowball-has-disproven-climate-change-once-and-for-all/>.

Bibliography

Canary Initiative. City of Aspen Colorado, n.d. Web. 14 Nov. 2015. <http://aspenpitkin.com/Living-in-the-Valley/Green-Initiatives/Canary-Initiative/>.

CDC. *Climate Change and Extreme Heat Events.* CDC, n.d. Web. 3 Oct. 2015 <http://www.cdc.gov/climateandhealth/pubs/ClimateChangeandExtremeHeatEvents.pdf>

Center for Sea Level Rise. Old Dominion University, n.d. Web. 14 Nov. 2015. <http://www.centerforsealevelrise.org/>.

Climate Change: Vital Signs of the Planet. Ed. Holly Shaftel. NASA, 29 Oct. 2015. Web. 30 Oct. 2015. <http://climate.nasa.gov>.

"Climate Change | WFP | United Nations World Food Programme - Fighting Hunger Worldwide." *World Food Programme.* WFP, n.d. Web. 14 Nov. 2015. <https://www.wfp.org/climate-change>.

"Climate Change." *World Health Organization.* WHO, n.d. Web. 5 Sept. 2015. <http://www.who.int/heli/risks/climate/climatechange/en/>.

"Climate Science and Solutions - POW." *Protect Our Winters.* PWO, n.d. Web. 10 Aug. 2015. <http://protectourwinters.org/climate-science-and-solutions/>.

"Committee on Adaptation to a Changing Climate." *American Society of Civil Engineers.* ASCE, n.d. Web. 15 Sept. 2015. <http://www.asce.org/climate-change/committee-on-adaptation-to-a-changing-climate/>.

"Current Issues Climate Policy." *ExxonMobil.* Exxon Mobil Corporation, n.d. Web. 1 Mar. 2015.

Bibliography

<http://corporate.exxonmobil.com/en/current-issues/climate-policy/climate-policy-principles/overview>.

Chan, Margaret, Director-General of the World Health Organization. "How Climate Change Can Rattle the Foundations of Public Health." *The Huffington Post*, 15 Sept. 2014. Web. 20 June 2015. <http://www.huffingtonpost.com/dr-margaret-chan/how-climate-change-can-ra_b_5822950.html>.

Chasing Ice. Dir. Jeff Orlowski. 2012. Film.

Clifford, Mark L. "China's Xi Jinping Announces Cap-and-Trade Carbon Program: Will It Work?" *Forbes Magazine*, 30 Sept. 2015. Web. 14 Nov. 2015. <http://www.forbes.com/sites/mclifford/2015/09/30/chinas-xi-jinping-announces-cap-and-trade-carbon-program-will-it-work/>.

Davenport, Coral. "Industry Awakens to Threat of Climate Change." *The New York Times*, 23 Jan. 2014. Web. 14 Nov. 2015. <http://www.nytimes.com/2014/01/24/science/earth/threat-to-bottom-line-spurs-action-on-climate.html>.

Disruption. Dir. Kelly Nyks & Jared P. Scott. 2014. Film.

Elfrink, Tim. "Sea Level Rise Threatens to Drown Miami Even Faster Than Feared, UM Researcher Finds." *Miami New Times*, 23 Feb. 2015. Web. 14 Sept. 2015. <http://www.miaminewtimes.com/news/sea-level-rise-threatens-to-drown-miami-even-faster-than-feared-um-researcher-finds-6537603>.

Elgie, Stewart. "British Columbia's Carbon Tax Shift: An Environmental and Economic Success." *Development in a Changing Climate: Making Our Future Sustainable*. The World Bank, 10 Oct. 2014. Web. 23 Nov. 2015. <http://blogs.worldbank.org/climatechange/british-

columbia-s-carbon-tax-shift-environmental-and-economic-success>.

Estrada, M. & Alexander, S. *San Diego County Key Influential Interviews on Climate Change Knowledge and Engagement, Summer of 2011*. University of San Diego, 2012.

Fox, Porter. "The End of Snow?" *The New York Times*, 07 Feb. 2014. Web. 10 Aug. 2015.
<http://www.nytimes.com/2014/02/08/opinion/sunday/the-end-of-snow.html?_r=1>.

Years of Living Dangerously. The Years Project. 13 Apr. 2014. TV and Itunes.
<http://yearsoflivingdangerously.com/>.

"Global Warming: What Should Be Done?" *The New York Times*. Stanford University, Resources for the Future, The New York Times, 28 Jan. 2015. Web. 26 Oct. 2015.
<http://www.nytimes.com/interactive/2015/01/29/us/global-warming-poll.html?_r=2>.

Giddens, Anthony. *The Politics of Climate Change*. Cambridge: Polity, 2009. Print.

Goldenberg, Suzanne. "World's Glaciers Melting at Accelerated Pace, Leading Scientists Say." *The Guardian*, 20 Jan. 2010. Web. 14 Nov. 2015.
<http://www.theguardian.com/environment/2010/jan/20/climate-change-glaciers-melting>.

Goodell, Jeff. "Goodbye, Miami." *Rolling Stone*, 20 June 2013. Web. 14 Sept. 2015.
<http://www.rollingstone.com/politics/news/why-the-city-of-miami-is-doomed-to-drown-20130620?page=2>.

Hagel, Chuck, United States Secretary of Defense. Speech. Conference of Defense Ministers of the Americas.

Bibliography

Peru, Arequipa. 13 Oct. 2014. Speech. U.S. Department of Defense, n.d. Web. 14 Nov. 2015. <http://www.defense.gov/News/Speeches/Speech-View/Article/605617>.

Henderson, Rebecca. *Making the Business Case for Environmental Sustainability*. Harvard Business School, 19 Feb. 2015. Web. Jun. 2015. <http://www.hbs.edu/faculty/Publication%20Files/15-068_c417331e-2146-40b6-8dfc-aa9a029db119.pdf>. Working paper.

IEA. *World Energy Investment Outlook: Special Report 2014*. Paris: IEA Publications, 2014. Web. 14 Nov. 2015. <http://www.iea.org/publications/freepublications/publication/WEIO2014.pdf>.

"Investor Network on Climate Risk (INCR)." *CERES*, n.d. Web. 14 Nov. 2015. <http://www.ceres.org/investor-network/incr>.

"IPCC, 2014: Climate Change 2014: Synthesis Report." Contribution of Working Groups I, II and III to the Fifth Assessment Report of the Intergovernmental Panel on Climate Change [Core Writing Team, R.K. Pachauri and L.A. Meyer (eds.)]. IPCC, Geneva, Switzerland, 151 pp. IPCC, n.d. Web, Aug. 2015. <http://ar5-syr.ipcc.ch/>.

Kaplan, Robert S., and David P. Norton. "Having Trouble with Your Strategy? Then Map It." *Harvard Business Review*, 01 Sept. 2000. Web. 14 Nov. 2015. <https://hbr.org/2000/09/having-trouble-with-your-strategy-then-map-it>.

Kim, Jim Yong. "World Bank Group President Jim Yong Kim Remarks at Davos Press Conference." World Economic Forum. Switzerland, Davos. 23 Jan. 2014. The World Bank News: Speeches & Transcripts, n.d. Web. 14

Bibliography

Nov. 2015.
<http://www.worldbank.org/en/news/speech/2014/01/23/wo
rld-bank-group-president-jim-yong-kim-remarks-at-davos-
press-conference>.

Kahneman, Daniel. *Thinking, Fast and Slow*. New York:
Farrar, Straus and Giroux, 2011. Print.

Korten, Tristram. "Florida Officials Needled over 'Climate
Change' Controversy." *Miami Herald*, 19 Mar. 2015. Web.
14 Nov. 2015.
<http://www.miamiherald.com/news/local/environment/artic
le15409031.html>.

Leiserowitz, A., Maibach, E., Roser-Renouf, C., Feinberg,
G. & Howe, P. *Global Warming's Six Americas, September
2012*. Yale University and George Mason University. New
Haven, CT: Yale Project on Climate Change
Communication, 2013.

Leiserowitz, A., Maibach, E., Roser-Renouf, C., Feinberg,
G., & Howe, P. *Climate Change in the American Mind:
Americans' Global Warming Beliefs and Attitudes in
September, 2012*. Yale University and George Mason
University. New Haven, CT: Yale Project on Climate
Change Communication, 2012.

Luckerson, Victor. "Tesla Model S Named Best Car for 2nd
Year in a Row." *Time*. Time Inc, Network, 24 Feb. 2015.
Web. 14 Nov. 2015. <http://time.com/3721049/tesla-
model-s-consumer-reports-car/>.

Mace, Georgina et al. *Resilience to Extreme Weather*. The
Royal Society, 2014.

Maibach, E., Leiserowitz, A., Roser-Renouf, C., Myers, T.,
Rosenthal, S. & Feinberg, G. *The Francis Effect: How
Pope Francis Changed the Conversation about Global
Warming*. George Mason University and Yale University.

Bibliography

Fairfax, VA: George Mason University Center for Climate Change Communication, 2015.

Marshall, George. *Don't Even Think about It: Why Our Brains Are Wired to Ignore Climate Change*. New York: Bloomsbury USA, 2014. Print.

McGlade, Christophe, and Paul Ekins. "The Geographical Distribution of Fossil Fuels Unused When Limiting Global Warming to 2°C." Nature 517 (2015): 187-90. 7 Jan. 2015. Web. Aug. 2015. <doi:10.1038/nature14016>.

McGrath, Matt. "Alaska Mulls Extra Oil Drilling to Cope with Climate Change." *BBC News*, 12 Oct. 2015. Web. 14 Sept. 2015. <http://www.bbc.com/news/science-environment-34501867>.

McGrath, Matt. "Warming Set to Breach 1C Threshold - BBC News." *BBC News*, 9 Nov. 2015. Web. 28 Nov. 2015. <http://www.bbc.com/news/science-environment-34763036>.

McNoldy, Brian. "During Autumn King Tides, Nuisance Flooding Becomes Chronic Flooding in Miami Area." The Washington Post, 20 Oct. 2015. Web. 29 Nov. 2015 <https://www.washingtonpost.com/news/capital-weather-gang/wp/2015/10/20/during-autumn-king-tides-nuisance-flooding-becomes-chronic-flooding-in-miami-area/>

McKinsey & Company. Greenhouse Gas Abatement Cost Curves. *McKinsey & Company*, n.d. Web. 14 Nov. 2015. <http://www.mckinsey.com/client_service/sustainability/latest_thinking/greenhouse_gas_abatement_cost_curves>.

Melillo, Jerry M., Terese (T.C.) Richmond, and Gary W. Yohe, Eds., 2014: *Climate Change Impacts in the United States: The Third National Climate Assessment. U.S. Global Change Research Program*, 841 pp. doi:10.7930/J0Z31WJ2.

Bibliography

Merchants of Doubt. Dir. Robert Kenner. 2014. Film.

Morales, Alex. "Climate Change to Hit Sovereign Creditworthiness: S&P." *Bloomberg*, 15 May 2014. Web. 14 Nov. 2015. <http://www.bloomberg.com/news/articles/2014-05-15/climate-change-to-hit-sovereign-creditworthiness-s-p>.

"More Than 100 Ski Areas Sign Climate Declaration, Calling for U.S. Policy Action on Climate Change." *CERES*. CERES, 29 May 2013. Web. 10 Aug. 2015. <http://www.ceres.org/press/press-releases/more-than-100-ski-areas-sign-climate-declaration-calling-for-u.s.-policy-action-on-climate-change#List>.

Moreno, Ivan. "Colo. Getting a Climate Change Czar." *The Denver Post*, 5 May 2013. Web. 14 Nov. 2015. <http://www.denverpost.com/news/ci_23354097/colo-getting-climate-change-czar>.

Mufson, Steven. "Shell Oil Will Drop Its Membership in ALEC, Citing Differences over Climate Change." *The Washington Post*, 7 Aug. 2015. Web. 30 Oct. 2015. <https://www.washingtonpost.com/news/post-politics/wp/2015/08/07/shell-oil-will-drop-its-membership-in-alec-citing-differences-over-climate-change/>.

"ND-GAIN Funded by Kresge Foundation to Develop U.S. Urban Adaptation Assessment." *University of Notre Dame News*. University of Notre Dame, 5 Jan. 2015. Web. 14 Nov. 2015. <http://news.nd.edu/news/54990-nd-gain-funded-by-kresge-foundation-to-develop-u-s-urban-adaptation-assessment/>.

"Notre Dame Global Adaptation Index (ND-GAIN)." *University of Notre Dame: Environmental Change Initiative*. University of Notre Dame, n.d. Web. 14 Nov. 2015. <http://www.gain.org/>.

Bibliography

"New FEMA Rules Troubling for GOP Governors Who Deny Climate Change." *The Washington Times*, 23 Mar. 2015. Web. 14 Nov. 2015. <http://www.washingtontimes.com/news/2015/mar/23/fema-rules-trouble-for-climate-change-deniers/>.

Parker, Laura. "Treading Water." *National Geographic*, Feb. 2015. Web. 14 Nov. 2015. <http://ngm.nationalgeographic.com/2015/02/climate-change-economics/parker-text>.

Paulson, Henry M, Jr. "The Coming Climate Crash." *The New York Times*, 21 June 2014. Web. 14 Nov. 2015. <http://www.nytimes.com/2014/06/22/opinion/sunday/lessons-for-climate-change-in-the-2008-recession.html?_r=2>.

PlaNYC. NYC Mayor's Office, n.d. Web. 14 Nov. 2015. <http://www.nyc.gov/html/planyc/html/home/home.shtml>.

"Resilience: Sustaining the Supply Chain." *PricewaterhouseCoopers LLP*, Jul. 2012. Web. 14 Nov 2015 <https://www.pwc.com/us/en/corporate-sustainability-climate-change/assets/pwc-sustaining-the-supply-chain-july-2012.pdf>.

Rigby, Claire. "Drought Drives Water Shortage to Critical Stage in Sao Paulo, Brazil." *Los Angeles Times*, 19 Aug. 2015. Web. 14 Nov. 2015. <http://www.latimes.com/world/brazil/la-fg-brazil-drought-20150820-story.html>.

Rising Tide. Prod. William Brangham. *Need to Know on PBS*. PBS, 27 Apr. 2012. Web. 14 Nov. 2015. <http://www.pbs.org/wnet/need-to-know/environment/rising-tide-in-norfolk-va/13739/>.

Bibliography

Risky Business | The Economic Risk of Climate Change in the US. Risky Business, n.d. Web. 26 Oct. 2015. <http://riskybusiness.org/>.

Rosenthal, Elisabeth. "Huff and Puff and Blow Your House Down." *The New York Times*, 12 Feb. 2011. Web. 15 Sept. 2015. <http://www.nytimes.com/2011/02/13/weekinreview/13rose nthal.html>.

Rusbridger, Alan. "The Argument for Divesting from Fossil Fuels Is Becoming Overwhelming." *The Guardian*, 16 Mar. 2015. Web. 26 Sept. 2015 <http://www.theguardian.com/environment/2015/mar/16/ar gument-divesting-fossil-fuels-overwhelming-climate-change>.

Schleifstein, Mark. "Louisiana Is Losing a Football Field of Wetlands an Hour, New U.S. Geological Survey Study Says." *The Times-Picayune*, 2 June 2011. Web. 14 Nov. 2015. <http://www.nola.com/environment/index.ssf/2011/06/louisi ana_is_losing_a_football.html>.

Schneider, Stephen H., William R. L. Anderegg, James W. Prall, and Jacob Harold. *Expert Credibility in Climate Change*. PNAS, 9 Apr. 2010. Web. 13 May 2015. <http://www.pnas.org/content/107/27/12107.full>.

Sea Level Rise and Coastal Flooding Impacts v2.0. U.S. National Oceanic and Atmospheric Administration, n.d. Web. 3 Oct. 2015. <https://coast.noaa.gov/slr/>.

Snowe, Olympia J. "Lack of Action on Climate Change Is Costing Fishing Jobs." *Newsweek*, 9 Feb. 2015. Web. 14 Nov. 2015. <http://www.newsweek.com/lack-action-climate-change-costing-fishing-jobs-305642>.

Bibliography

"Special Report: Climate Change." *The Economist*, 28 Nov. 2015 - 4 Dec. 2015. Print

Stern, N. H. *A Blueprint for a Safer Planet: How to Manage Climate Change and Create a New Era of Progress and Prosperity*. London: Bodley Head, 2009. Print.

Stokes, B. Wike, R. Carle, J. *Global Concern About Climate Change, Broad Support for Limiting Emissions*. Pew Research Center, 2015.

"The Curious Case of El Niño." *ClearPath Foundation*, n.d. Web. 14 Nov. 2015. <http://www.clearpath.org/en/latest/more-featured-stories/curious-case-of-el-nino.html>.

The Kresge Foundation Programs Environment. The Kresge Foundation, n.d. Web. 14 Nov. 2015. <http://kresge.org/programs/environment>.

"The World Set Free." *Cosmos: A Spacetime Odyssey*. Dir. Brannon Braga. Fox. 1 June 2014. Netflix.

Toffel, Michael, and Auden Schendler. "Corporate Leaders Need to Step Up on Climate Change." *HBS Working Knowledge*. Harvard Business School, 05 June 2013. Web. 14 Nov. 2015. <http://hbswk.hbs.edu/item/corporate-leaders-need-to-step-up-on-climate-change>.

United States. Department of Defense. Office of the Deputy Under Secretary of Defense for Installations and Environment. *2014 Climate Change Adaptation Roadmap*. Department of Defense, June 2014. Web. 15 Nov. 2015 <http://www.acq.osd.mil/ie/download/CCARprint_wForeword_c.pdf>.

United States. Department of the Army. U.S. Army Corps of Engineers. *Sea-Level Change Considerations for Civil Works Programs*. Circular No. 1165-2-212. 1 Oct. 2011.

Web 23 Sept. 2015
<http://planning.usace.army.mil/toolbox/library/ECs/EC116
52212Nov2011.pdf>

United States. Securities and Exchange Commission.
*Commission Guidance Regarding Disclosure Related to
Climate Change*. By Elizabeth M. Murphy. SEC, 8 Feb.
2010. Web. 3 Oct. 2015
<https://www.sec.gov/rules/interp/2010/33-9106.pdf>.
[Release Nos. 33-9106; 34-61469; FR-82]

Van Beurden, Ben, Chief Executive Officer, Royal Dutch
Shell, plc. "Working Together to Build a Lower Carbon,
Higher Energy Future." Center on Global Energy Policy at
Columbia University, New York City. Speech. 2 Sept.
2014. Shell, n.d. Web. 5 Jun. 2015.
<http://www.shell.com/global/aboutshell/media/speeches-
and-articles/2014/working-together-lower-carbon-higher-
energy.html>.

Van Beurden, Ben. "Why This 'Big Oil' CEO Believes In
Applying A Price To Carbon." *Forbes Magazine*, 23 Sept.
2014. Web. 14 Nov. 2015.
<http://www.forbes.com/sites/sciencebiz/2014/09/23/why-
this-big-oil-ceo-believes-in-applying-a-price-to-carbon/>.

"Weather-Related Loss & Damage Rising as Climate
Warms." *The World Bank News*. The World Bank, 18 Nov.
2013. Web. 20 Sept. 2015.
<http://www.worldbank.org/en/news/feature/2013/11/18/dis
aster-climate-resilience-in-a-changing-world>.

Winston, Andrew S. *The Big Pivot: Radically Practical
Strategies for a Hotter, Scarcer, and More Open World*.
Cambridge: Harvard Business Review Press, 2014. Print.

"World's Leading Institutional Investors Managing $24
Trillion Call for Carbon Pricing, Ambitious Global Climate
Deal." *CERES*. CERES, 18 Sept. 2014. Web. 14 Nov.

Bibliography

2015. <http://www.ceres.org/press/press-releases/world2019s-leading-institutional-investors-managing-24-trillion-call-for-carbon-pricing-ambitious-global-climate-deal>.

Yergin, Daniel. *The Quest: Energy, Security and the Remaking of the Modern World*. New York: Penguin, 2011. Print.

Zurayk, Rami. "Use Your Loaf: Why Food Prices Were Crucial in the Arab Spring." *The Guardian*, 16 July 2011. Web. 13 Sept. 2015. <http://www.theguardian.com/lifeandstyle/2011/jul/17/bread-food-arab-springhttp://www.theguardian.com/lifeandstyle/2011/jul/17/bread-food-arab-spring>.

Bibliography

Additional Resources:

adaptationnow.com
c40.org
cakex.org
carbontrust.com
cdp.net/en-US/Pages/HomePage.aspx
centerforsealevelrise.org
ceres.org
citizensclimatelobby.org
cleanenergyworksforus.org
clearpath.org
climate.gov
climate.nasa.gov
climateaction2020.unfccc.int
climatedata.us
climatenexus.org
climateoutreach.org
earthinstitute.columbia.edu
edf.org/climate
energysavingtrust.org.uk
environment.nationalgeographic.com/environment/global-warming
environment.yale.edu/climate-communication
epa.gov/climatechange
floodofvoices.tumblr.com
gofossilfree.org
icleiusa.org
index.gain.org
interfaithpowerandlight.org
iseechange.org
maps.coastalresilience.org
masssave.com
mothersoutfront.org
nature.org/ourinitiatives/urgentissues/global-warming-climate-change
nca2014.globalchange.gov
ncdc.noaa.gov/stormevents
protectourwinters.org

Additional Resources

riskybusiness.org
rmi.org
royalsociety.org/topics-policy/energy-environment-climate
skepticalscience.com
staycool4grandkids.org
theguardian.com/environment/climate-change,
thesolutionsproject.org
toolkit.climate.gov
topics.wsj.com/subject/G/global-warming/1660
tyndall.ac.uk
unfccc.int/2860.php
usa.gov/elected-officials
withouthotair.com
worldbank.org/en/topic/climatechange
worldwildlife.org/initiatives/climate
wri.org/our-work/topics/climate
yearsoflivingdangerously.com
100resilientcities.org
350.org

Made in the USA
Middletown, DE
30 March 2016